MARX, LENIN
AND THE
SCIENCE OF REVOLUTION

MARX, LENIN
AND THE
SCIENCE *of* REVOLUTION

BY

MAX EASTMAN

HYPERION PRESS, INC.
WESTPORT, CONNECTICUT

Library of Congress Cataloging in Publication Data

Eastman, Max, 1883-1969.
Marx, Lenin, and the science of revolution.

Reprint of the 1926 ed. published by G. Allen &
Unwin, London.
Includes bibliographical references.
1. Socialism. 2. Marx, Karl, 1818-1883.
3. Lenin, Vladimir Il'ich, 1870-1924.
4. Revolutions. I. Title.
HX56.E3 1973   335.43   73-838
ISBN 0-88355-034-2

Published in 1926
by George Allen & Unwin, Ltd., London, England

First Hyperion reprint edition 1973

Library of Congress Catalogue Number 73-838

ISBN 0-88355-034-2

Printed in the United States of America

PREFACE

THIS book is the principal fruit of a visit to Soviet Russia. It is also the completion of a task which I began ten years ago in a series of articles in " The Masses " called " Towards Liberty, The Method of Progress ". I was deterred from finishing those articles by many things, but chiefly by my ignorance of the international literature of Marxism. During my visit to Russia I succeeded in reducing the proportions of this ignorance. I also became convinced that nothing I could do is more important than to finish that task. It now entails a criticism of certain phases of the revolutionary dictatorship in Russia, but I trust it will be obvious that this criticism is sympathetic, and in no sense a political attack.

MAX EASTMAN.

CONTENTS

PART II

THE SCIENCE OF REVOLUTIONARY ENGINEERING

PART I

THE PHILOSOPHY OF MARXISM

CHAPTER I

THE FUNCTION OF THINKING

IT seems evident that conscious thought developed in the course of evolution only when it became needful as a means of survival. Desire in its simple nature is undefined and unconscious, and the lower forms of life satisfy their desires by continuing in a state of random activity, until they come by chance into bodily contact with a satisfaction. Higher forms of life develop feelers with specialized sensitivity, which enable them to explore the environment without submitting their whole body to danger. They develop organs of smell and sight and hearing which enable them to detect a satisfaction, or apprehend a danger, at a considerable distance in space and time. And it is in connection with these organs that the value of a conscious act of perception begins to be apparent. For the essence of such perception is the interpretation of a present fragment of sensation upon the basis of past experience. The smell of food is not food, and the sight of danger is not dangerous. But if by virtue of memory and imagination, the smell of food *means* food, and the sight of danger *means* danger, then the organism can satisfy itself or escape, without making in each case a complete experiment.

But even here it cannot learn anything new except by the method of random experimentation—by the method, that is, of trying out in action every meaning that is suggested. And thought, in so far as it is distinguished from the mere act of perception, is distinguished by a moment of suspense during which the suggested meaning, or more than one suggested meaning, is tried out inside the head. Thought is tentative action ; it is action in the process of formation. It is adjustment, delayed in order that it may perfect itself and relate itself with safety to a larger and more complex environment.[1]

Some such conception of the origin and nature of thought, is forced upon the genetic psychologist, not only by the central tendency of biological science, but by an experimental study of the intelligence of infants and animals. Indeed the very employment of experiment in these fields, implies an instrumental conception of intelligence. For it is only by setting before the infant or the animal a goal of desire, and observing his efforts to attain it, that any experiment can be made.

Moreover, if we study in our own minds any simple example of thinking, we are led to a similar conception. We button our clothes unconsciously so long as all is in order and the process goes smoothly to its end ; but if a button is missing, we become conscious of the process, and we think. And our thinking takes a form corresponding to the situation in which it arose. It is an interpretation of the factual difficulty in the light of the desired end, a trying out in imagination of plans which

[1] It is the method of some psychologists to regard all intelligent functions as completely fulfilled by the higher nerve-centres, and conscious thought as a mere accidental by-product of the proceeding—or even to deny conscious thought any "scientific" existence at all. This is one of those over-simplifications of fact, usually advertised as the highest blossom of the scientific spirit, but which are in reality the survival of a metaphysical taste for unity and the absolute. The fact underlying this metaphysic is that conscious thought performs a far smaller function in the process of nervous adjustment, and performs it less frequently, than men have been in the habit of believing.

spontaneously suggest themselves for arriving at the end on the basis of the existing facts.

What complicates this process, and gives rise to so many problems about thinking, is a certain disposition men have to exercise this function for its own sake— their pleasure in meditation, and their instinctive curiosity, which make the mere definition of facts itself a desired end. The people who first studied thought, and advanced theories about it, were themselves very strong in this disposition and instinct. They were great meditators, great investigators. And so naturally they imagined that thought in its original and most general form is pure meditation, or a perfectively disinterested attempt to define facts. It is so far from this, that we may even ask the question whether pure meditation is very different from pure day-dreaming, and whether it is possible to define a fact of any complexity, and prove that the definition is valid, except in relation to some purposive activity. At least it is with an organ formed to function as an integral part of purposive activities that we meditate ; it is with an instrument of interest that we seek to satisfy our disinterested curiosity. Working hypotheses are the original form of its knowledge, and experimental verification is originally its only " truth ".

A recognition of this fact involves one of the profoundest changes that has ever occurred in the history of science ; and it would be absurd to pretend that the change is already accomplished, or that half the difficulties arising out of the genetic view of human thinking have been met and overcome. A scientific Logic—an account of the technique of all science, which shall itself be but a practical application of the science of psychology, in accord with a developed physiology of the nervous system—is still only a reasonable dream. But it is one of the most reasonable dreams that science ever dreamed. And no one in touch with the facts, and free from the prejudices arising from religion or idealistic metaphysics, can deny that it is in process of development, and that certain of its outlines are already visible.

The simplest perception contains an element of immediate sense experience, and an element of mental interpretation that is purposive. The highest scientific thinking seems merely to delay the union of these two. On its inductive side it examines the existing experience ; on its deductive side it develops the implications of the interpretive idea ; it tests the applicability of the one to the other ; and it ceases, normally, when an adequate general human adjustment is reached.

This instrumental interpretation of consciousness, the fruit of that biological psychology founded by Charles Darwin, has received corroboration of late years from a science which developed in almost complete independence of it—the psychology of the clinic. The therapeutic importance of *becoming conscious* is the essence of the discovery made by Sigmund Freud in the sphere of functional nervous and mental disease. Such disease is, according to Freud, the result of conflicts between different powerful motives in our nature—sexual motives for the most part, and motives of primitive egoism, conflicting with motives arising out of our social self-consciousness. These conflicts may never have been conscious, or they may have been conscious at one time, and been resolved by suppressing into unconsciousness the socially unacceptable motive. That motive does not perish by thus returning to the original condition of all life, but continues there in the organism, self-active and dynamic, and it finds expression in spite of the more acceptable motive which occupies the field of consciousness. It finds expression through rationalization and

" substitution " in the first place—falsifying our conscious thoughts in such a way that we can pursue its ends under the guise of a more respectable motive. It finds expression in dreams, in little slips and errors of everyday life, in wit and humour, in poetry and myth. And with unstable or wounded natures, it finds expression in all the innumerable symptoms of hysteria, and functional nervous and mental disease.

That is the Freudian theory, expressed in a not too narrowly Freudian way. And the Freudian treatment, psycho-analysis, consists of a varied and prolonged, but yet very simple and natural effort to make the patient conscious of his own real desires. When he has become conscious of them, the ordinary process of thought and its education, is the only cure that is offered. The cure is occasionally almost instantaneous, because the suppressed motive is infantile, and its irrelevance to the present situation is immediately recognized. At other times it is very slow, and often it is unattainable. But in any case it involves nothing more mysterious than the original natural function of all conscious thought—the adjustment of a dynamic organism to a complex environment.

In treating this organism as dynamic—as a thing seeking stimuli, instead of merely responding to them—Freud made a considerable departure from the traditional psychology. In the traditional psychology, thought appears as an instrument for guiding " reactions ". In the Freudian way of talking, it is an instrument for defining " desires ", or resolving the conflicts between them. In both cases, however, it remains an instrument ; and Freud's way of talking is only closer to the evolutionary view of organic functions in general. His influence upon the development of a scientific logic will be but a further extension of the influence of Darwin.

Darwin's influence destroyed for all matter-of-fact scientific minds the metaphysical pretensions of human thought. If thought in its origin and biological development consists in the purposive interpretation of one part of the experienced world in terms of others, the probability that it can, in the brains of the professional philosophers, fly entirely free of its original nature and essence, and give us a non-interpretive account or picture of Being-at-Large, and its ways and meanings independent of our life purposes, is exceedingly small. And even if that gymnastic is possible, it can be achieved only by recognizing the purposive element in all cases of thinking where it can possibly be detected or imagined, and confining those professional philosophers to the dryest, and most unbeautiful, and unmoral, and unpolitical, and unpaid-for manipulation of algebraic formulæ. In the meantime, which is likely to be forever, the highest kind of thinking and the most " scientific ", is not that which makes the most grandiose pretence to universality, but that which most carefully and candidly acknowledges the specific problem out of which it arose, and the purpose which made that specific thing a problem. That is the intellectual outcome of Darwin's application of the idea of evolution to organic life. It is the establishment of a new kind of humble scientific candour—an attitude which may be described as affirmative scientific scepticism. And Freud reinforces it, by showing that this state of candour cannot be achieved by acknowledging merely those motives of which our social dignity permits us to become conscious, but that we must assume, in the absence of any express effort to the contrary, that our thoughts are a disguised instrument for the attainment of ends we have no knowledge of.

CHAPTER II

THE MARXIAN PSYCHOLOGY

THERE were many anticipators of the functional view of intelligence, and among them Karl Marx deserves a distinguished place. In his " Theses on Feuerbach ", Marx made several statements which sound like the foundation of an instrumental logic.

" The chief fault of all materialism heretofore," he said, " including Feuerbach's, is that the object, reality, the sensible, is understood only under the form of object, or of contemplation ; not as human sensory activity, practice, not subjectively. Hence it has come about that the active side has been developed in opposition to materialism by idealism . . ."

" Feuerbach . . . does not understand the sensible as practical human-sensory activity."

" Feuerbach considers only the theoretical attitude as the truly human, while practice is grasped and defined merely in the dirty-Jew aspect of phenomenon. Feuerbach therefore does not understand the significance of the ' revolutionary ', of practical-critical action."

" In practice man must prove the truth—that is, the reality and power, the this-worldliness, of his thoughts."

" Philosophers have merely interpreted the world in various ways ; the thing is to change it."

It seems in these fragments as though Marx were rejecting entirely the " spectator theory " of knowledge, and adopting the attitude of genetic psychology, with all its distrust of the pretences of metaphysics. If sensation itself is " practical ", and if thought at its best is " practical-critical action ", and if even philosophy is not rightly an interpretation of the world, but an operation upon it—there is certainly little to add, in order to arrive at the attitude which I have called affirmative scepticism.

In spite of these wise sayings, however, Marx did not arrive at that scientific attitude. He did not escape from the " spectator theory " of knowledge, nor abandon any of the essential pretences of metaphysics. And the exact reason is that these wise sayings were not with him simple observations of fact. They were not the foundation of an enquiry. Marx's recognition of the practical in sensation, and of the instrumental function of thinking, was an inference which he thought it possible to make from a philosophy of the universe in which he already believed. And that philosophy of the universe was founded—although Marx never happened to notice it— upon an exactly opposite view of the nature of sensation, and of the function of thinking.

Marx believed, as a young man, in the philosophy of Hegel. And Hegel's philosophy depends upon the assumption that the practical element in our consciousness is merely accidental or apparent, a thing to be dismissed entirely if we wish really to understand the mind.

" If the activities of mind," he says, " are treated as mere manifestations, forces, perhaps in terms stating their utility or suitability for some other interest of head or heart, there is no indication of the true final aim of the whole business. That can only be the intelligible unity of mind, and its activity can only have itself as aim ; i.e. its aim can only be to . . . reach and get hold of itself, and to liberate itself to itself. . . . This is the only rational mode of studying the mind and its various activities."

" Thought is the universal in all the acts of conception and recollection ; in short, in every mental activity, in willing, wishing and the like. All these faculties are only further specializations of thought."

" If in pursuance of the foregoing remarks we consider Logic to be the system of the pure types of thought, we find that the. . . Philosophy of Mind takes the place, as it were, of an Applied Logic . . . Its problem is only to recognize the logical forms under the shapes they assume in . . . Mind —shapes which are only a particular mode of expression for the forms of pure thought."

That is the psychology of Hegel. He believed that the real nature of intelligence and the explanation of all consciousness, is to be discovered by examining the relation between the categories of pure logic. It is to be discovered by examining those concepts which are the most remote in point of generality and abstraction from the experience of concrete things—*being*, *becoming*, *quantity*, *number*, and so forth. The instinctive movement of the mind—and particularly of the Hegelian mind, which has a strong taste for paradox—among these remote abstractions is, according to Hegel, " the principle and very unadulterated self of mind ". That is, you see, as far away as you can possibly get from a real science of the mind—from studying mind in its origin and development. Hegel begins at formal Logic, at the very top. And lest there should be a danger of somebody else going up higher, he allows you to know that it is not even logic really that he is talking about, but a kind of special Hegelian Super-Logic, a semi-intelligible esoteric craft of the metaphysical high-priest, which can alone give you the true science of thought, and the true explanation of what consciousness is, and what it is for.

The essence of this esoteric craft, as it developed in the hands of that master magician, was first to convince you that these remote abstractions are not necessarily abstract. They all may seem to be abstract in mere psychology, or even in logic, but as they reappear in the inner shrine of the Hegelian Higher Logic, the most general terms are concrete. And moreover they are alive and moving. The motion of your mind among them is really a participation in their self-active motion. And it is a motion of a very peculiar kind, to which Hegel gave the name of " Dialectic ". It is an assertion of something, and then a passing over into its opposite, or a negation of that something by itself, and then a " negation of the negation ", or reconciliation of these two opposites in a higher unity which includes them both. And all the motion in the world, both in nature and human history, is—if you will examine it with a sufficiently casuistical determination to believe so, and particularly if you will refrain from defining exactly what you mean by " opposite "—a motion of this same kind. It is an evolution by contradiction and the reconciliation of " opposites ". In fact the very existence of the world is such a performance. For the world is really composed of a process of thought, but this process of thought—the Idea, which is another name for God— negates itself in the world of matter, and then " negates the negation " by evolving the human mind out of that matter.

That is the Hegelian philosophy—or at least that is the Hegelian philosophy as it appears to me. I do not imagine that anybody else will agree with me, and I must add that it is one of the most indubitable virtues of this philosophy that nobody can find out exactly what it is. Hegelism is like a mental disease—you cannot know what it is until you get it, and then you can't know because you've got it. Suffice it to say that Marx believed throughout his young manhood in some such philosophy as I have described. And he was awakened out of this mystical condition by Ludwig Feuerbach, who having been a Hegelian, became a man of simple good sense, and said that the world is not really composed of a process of thought, but it is composed of things, and the process of thought is something which goes on only inside a man's head. Engels describes the " rapture " with which Marx and he greeted Feuerbach. He says that no one who had not lived through it, could possibly imagine the " liberating effect " that his writings had upon them. And from that you can imagine their previous state of hypnosis, the degree of their captivity to the thought-conjurings of the High-Priest of the Idea.

Their captivity had indeed been so complete that neither Marx nor Engels felt entirely at ease in the new universe to which Feuerbach introduced them. They felt the lack of something in this universe—the lack of a " dynamic principle ", as Marx's biographer describes it. They wanted to know that this material world is a going thing, just like the ideal world in which they had been brought up, and they wanted to know how it is going. Feuerbach could not tell them that. And so, instead of simply observing as a matter of evident fact that it *is* going, and taking up the long experimental-scientific labour of finding out how it is going in various specific parts, they went back to Hegel and got a piece of philosophy that would tell them how it is going abstractly, and universally, in advance of investigation, and without genuine verification. They went back and got the " Dialectic ". They declared that this mystical idea of progress by contradiction and the reconciliation of opposites, is still a true and universal law of motion both in human thought and in the material universe. Hegel's only mistake had been to imagine that the dialectic process belongs originally to mind—to an Absolute and Divine mind—and that the motions of the material world are an alien reflection of it. On the contrary, they said, it belongs originally to matter, which is the fundamental reality, and it reappears in our human minds, because our brains are nothing but an apparatus for making mental reflections of this world of matter. . . . That is the philosophy of " dialectic materialism ", the intellectual background of scientific socialism, and since the proletarian revolution in Russia, the official state philosophy of the Union of Soviet Socialist Republics.

It is clear that this philosophy does not, and cannot, alter in the slightest degree the *psychology* of Hegel—his fundamental general account of what the mind is, and how it should be studied. Dialectic Materialism declares that the world is essentially material, and that mind evolved out of matter in connection with the complex organization of the central nervous system in animals and men. But it does not, and dare not, go on and say that the motions of this mind are a continuation of the motion of matter in that central nervous system, adaptive and practical motions, to be studied from the standpoint of Biology and Physiology rather than Logic. For, studied from this standpoint and in their actuality in concrete cases, these motions will be found to be not essentially logical—much less " dialectic "—and the whole vast mystic-intellectual legend of Hegel will fall to the ground altogether. As Hegel himself said, " To see that thought in its very nature is dialectical " is a " lesson of logic ". And the moment logic is cast down from its position as a factual account of what thought in its " inner essence " really is, and recognized to be a set of rules which men have made for the better employment of their thoughts, that moment this " lesson of logic " will lose its validity.

It will not lose its validity, for it never had any. But it will lose the possibility of obscuring and confusing the boldest political minds of five generations of mankind with an unintelligible mixture of emotional mysticism and psychological half-truth. Certainly nobody will contend that a dialectic philosophy of the universe could survive without Hegel's Logic, upon the sole basis of his Philosophy of Nature and History, and of such desultory empirical observations as he and his disciples occasionally bring to the support of it. A dialectic philosophy of the universe—whether it is materialistic or idealistic—stands or falls with Hegel's fundamental science of the mind. It stands or falls with the belief that " the principle and very unadulterated self of the mind " is to be found, not by examining its simple and practical beginnings, but by winding oneself all up in its most complicated and hypercultivated manifestation, where it has become an end in itself, and where its end is " to reach and get hold of itself and liberate itself to itself "—whatever in honest fact that may mean. Marx's philosophy of " Dialectic Materialism " is inextricably bound up with this old-fashioned way of studying the mind.

Marx himself used to describe his philosophy by saying that he had merely turned the philosophy of Hegel " right side up "—retaining the idea of dialectic evolution, that is, but putting matter instead of mind at the basis of it. He declared that he had thus got rid of the " mystical ", and retained the " rational " in the Hegelian system. But in order to get rid of the mystical in the Hegelian system, it would be necessary to turn Hegel's conception of *thought* right side up—to recognize that not Higher-Logic, and not logic, and not even pure psychology, but biological and physiological psychology will ultimately tell us what we can know about thought. And when you have done that, you will have none of Hegel's philosophy left ; you will be entirely purged of mysticism. And then, if you state that sensation is not contemplation but " human sensory activity ", and that thought at its best is " practical-critical action ", and that the business of philosophy is not to interpret the world but to change it, these statements will have an entirely different meaning from what they had in Marx's " Theses on Feuerbach ". They will mean the impossibility, or at least the entire improbability, of your thought's doing anything—leaving out art and poetry—but adjusting you to specific parts of the world, and adjusting them to you. It will mean that the way to think clearly is to acknowledge the practical—that is, specifically purposive —element in your own thinking.

Marx's very wise and modern sayings in the " Theses on Feuerbach " were an expression of his temperament, which was more that of a practical engineer than a metaphysician. Marx himself did not want to go to the school where he received his Hegelian education. His first taste of Hegel repelled him. His youthful instincts were against it, and his whole scientific life shows the struggle of those practical and realistic instincts against that education. Only thus can you explain his endless inability to finish what he began to write, and the vague obscurity of what he did write when it was theoretical. He struggled against his education, but his education triumphed. His philosophy, as it was finally formulated, leaves no place for the assertion that thought is a practical activity. It depends absolutely upon the Hegelian assumption that thought in its essence is not practical but " pure ", and that all the other activities of the mind—even " willing, wishing and the like "—are but " modes of expression of the forms of pure thought ".

It is not impossible that if Marx had devoted his mature mind to a re-statement of Hegel's logic, as he once contemplated doing, he might have confronted this inconsistency. He might have arrived at a real science of human intelligence, which would have swept the last vestiges of Hegelism out of him. He devoted himself to economics instead, and he left to Engels the task of formulating their common philosophy. Engels had neither the inventive genius nor the depth of intellectual conscience that Marx had, and his writings show no sense of the challenge to Hegelian psychology contained in the " Theses on Feuerbach ". All the forms of consciousness are for Engels mere automatic portraits of material reality, and their practicality is not a quality in them—it is merely an evidence that they are pictorially accurate. The motion of consciousness is to him not a dynamic, but a rational motion, factually described by the rules of the Hegelian logic ; and this motion also is but a " reflection " of the motion of nature.

That is the extent of the Marxian psychology as it appears in the writings of Engels. And up to the time of the Russian revolution this psychology took no single step forward. The greatest theorists of Marxism seem to have been as unaware of the development of a genetic and experimental science of the mind, as though it had taken place on another planet. Lafargue in an essay on " The Origin of the Ideas of Justice and the Good ", draws his authority from no psychologist later than Hobbes and Locke. Plekhanov, four years after the publication of James's Psychology, dismissed with a derisive phrase the idea of a science of human nature. Kautsky, assigning to Marx his position among the sciences, mentions the existence of a natural science of psychology, but only in order to run away from it and forget it. Lenin, although he was the incarnation of purposive thinking, was satisfied to describe all the dynamic activities of his mind as an automatic " repro- duction ", " copy ", " reflection "—and in one place he even says " photograph "—of the self-active motions of the material world.   Never was the " spectator theory " of knowledge reduced to a more perfect absurdity than on the lips of Lenin.   Never was it expressed in a nakeder form.   " Consciousness in general reflects exist- ence . . . social consciousness reflects social existence " —that is the extent of Lenin's psychology.   It must be said to his credit that he felt a certain weakness or want of specification in this formula, but his way of supplying the want was no better than that of Marx himself.   He recommended—but never began—a " systematic study of the Hegelian dialectic from the materialist point of view ".

The Russian revolution set free a great body of Marxian theorists, and theorists willing to become Marxian, if only from the pure love of theory.   It supplied them with publishing facilities, and encouraged them to take possession of the whole field of science in the name of Dialectic Materialism.   Naturally the science of psycho- logy did not escape this invasion.   It was approached— with somewhat the same mixture of caution and con- tempt with which one approaches a poisonous reptile— and a certain preliminary investigation was begun. Enough progress has been made to indicate what an orthodox " Marxian Psychology " will be, when it is fully developed.   It will be exactly what psychology was, what it had to be, with Hegel—a pious search among concrete states of consciousness, and in the books of real science which describe them, for that mystic abstract " essence " of the motion of pure thought called " Dialectic ".

A series of articles by a communist professor, K. Kornilov, described as " A First Reconnoitre in the Field of Psychology from the Marxian View-Point ", may serve as an example.   Kornilov takes his start from the statement of Engels that " dialectic is the universal law of motion in thought ", as well as in the external world. He seeks out various instances of motion described by contemporary psychology, which can be made to appear as examples of this " law ". He shows that the reflex arc has a natural kinship with the " triads " of Hegel, and that Freud's psycho-analytic release of a suppressed desire is an instance of the " reconciliation of opposites "—the desire and the motive suppressing it—in a " higher unity ". He describes how in sensation, according to Fechner's law, " quantity turns into quality "—and reminds us that this is one of the forms of the " Negation of the Negation ". There is nothing more fruitful in his articles than this desultory search for chance illustrations of that Hegelian formula. And there is nothing more fruitful in any of the articles which have followed this " first reconnoitre ".

There is, however, one point of hope in the work of these Soviet psychologists. For owing to the fact that Marx took the first step away from Hegel, declaring the primary thing in the world to be moving matter, they are necessarily opposed to the " subjectivist " attitude. They instinctively adhere to the attitude of Pavlov and Bechterev, who both consider the study of " reflexes ", or " reactions ", and the creation of a physiology of the higher nerve-centres, to be a primary task of psychology. And from the study of reflexes as the primary task of psychology to the conception of thought as a delayed reflex, and thus essentially an instrument of adjustment to particular realities, and not an irrelevant picture of reality at large, is a short step. It seems inevitable that the Marxian psychologists will take this step in due course of time.

The impossibility of remaining in the present position is well illustrated in that same series of articles by

Kornilov. After finishing his reconnoitre in various bypaths, Kornilov takes up what he calls the fundamental problem of the Stream of Consciousness. He says that the theory of the Association of Ideas has been inadequate to explain the motion of this stream, and that this problem remains to be solved by the " dialectic method ". " The fundamental principle of the movement of psychic life may yet be discovered ", he says, " and just by way of applying the dialectic method in the sphere of psychic life ".

Forgetting that the dialectic *is* the fundamental principle of the movement of psychic life—forgetting that Hegel has already discovered and decreed that all mental activities are only " a mode of expression of the forms of pure thought ", and that " we have but to let the thought-forms follow the impulse of their own organic life ", in order to see that every one " naturally veers round into its opposite "—forgetting that this complete analysis and revelation by Hegel of the fundamental principle of the movement of psychic life is the sole ground and reason-for-being of the " dialectic method," this Marxian psychology will now proceed to employ the " dialectic method " in order to *investigate* the *unsolved problem* of how the psychic life moves ! The impossibility of this position must come home to somebody sometime—but it may not be soon, for a State Philosophy is almost as heavy and paralysing a thing as a State Religion.

Among the extremer devotees of dialectic materialism in Russia, the very word psychology is denounced as bourgeois and counter-revolutionary. And these devotees imagine that what they are defending so fanatically is the materialism of Marx, and that they want to put physiology in the place of psychology. What they are defending is the dialectic of Marx, which stands or falls with our willingness to put logic in the place of psychology. And to put logic in the place of psychology is the fundamental trick of the idealist philosophers. You will find if you read him, that Hegel himself had the same phobia of an empirical, and especially a genetic, science of psychology. He insisted with continual anxiety upon the vast abyss between the rational faculties of man and the intelligence of " brutes ". It was as though he knew that this universal evolution, the child of his logic, would finally prove capable of devouring its mother.

Not only the prior thing in the world is matter and not mind, but the prior thing in mind is impulse and not reason. Those are the two steps away from " philosophy ", of which Marx took one. He might, if he had turned his mature mind to philosophic problems, have taken the other. But he did not do so. And it is necessary for those who want to develop the revolutionary science, and not merely defend it, to complete this movement of liberation.

CHAPTER III

THE BELIEF IN DIALECTIC MATERIALISM

A FUNCTIONAL science of the mind not only makes us sceptical of philosophical pretenses, but it enables us to begin to understand this peculiar process called " philosophy ", and explain what it really is. And since Marxism is a philosophy, that is obviously a first step towards understanding Marxism.

In primitive culture it is possible to distinguish two quite different kinds of thinking—animistic thinking, in which one tries to adjust oneself to the external world as to a person, and the ordinary practical thinking by which the daily arts of life are carried on. Animistic thinking consists essentially in trying by some sort of hocus-pocus to transfer your own wishes into the external world, and so get them realized. It is emotional and ceremonial and soon becomes institutionalized in the religious festivals, the Mysteries, the Priests, the Church. And because of its emotional hold upon men, it is taken in charge by the ruling and exploiting classes, and becomes the guardian of custom and " good morals ", and the chief cultural instrument for the maintenance of the *status quo*. It is aristocratic thinking, and makes up in elaboration and social standing for what it lacks in convincing force.

But the practical arts of life develop alongside of it, and indeed within its very temple, and the actual control of man over his environment begins to be almost as exciting as this rather monotonous conjuring of the world-spirit. Moreover these arts develop a technology which rests upon theoretic assumptions, and these theoretic assumptions begin to be formulated by creative. minds in contact with the artisan class. Men appear who dare to say that the world really *is* what the artisan assumes it to be in his daily work. And they come into conflict —whether as materialists, sceptics, Sophists, Socratic exasperating questioners, or what not—with the ceremonial, soulful, socially-authoritarian world-view. They are not philosophers, except in a very negative sense of the word. They are people who are satisfied with the assumptions of science and the arts. And they are satisfied because their interest is in doing things with the world, rather than in establishing a comfortable relation with its spirit.

It is obvious that these people are dangerous to the ruling powers, and it is in their ranks that we find the first great martyrs of science—Anaxagoras banished, Protagoras persecuted and tried for his life, Socrates put to death protesting that true piety is obedience to the laws of the state. The crime of Socrates was deeper than disobedience to the laws of the state. It was disobedience to the laws of animistic thinking. It was asking irreverent questions about the soul of man, and the definite meaning of those large emotional ideas which have the support of custom and the priests. Indeed I can think of no more revolutionary or dangerous idea than this one of Socrates, that piety is nothing but obedience to the laws of the state. Give us an equally irreverent definition of the state, and where are we, if not in the heart of Bolshevism ? It is obvious that such matter-of-fact people must be done away with. It is obvious, moreover, since those arts and sciences from which they derive their authority are going right on developing and attracting interest, that putting them to death is not going to be enough. They must be met on their own field and refuted. And for this a new and specially honourable and arduous kind of " speculative thinking " is required.

That, it seems to me, is the principal origin of " philosophy ", in the sense in which we are using the word. As the practical work of the mind advances, religion weakens, the priest loses his authority. Then the metaphysician steps forward and builds a home for the soul out of the very instruments of that practical work of the mind. Those instruments are, in the main, the logical categories—being, becoming, quantity, number, and so forth. The task of the metaphysician, speaking very broadly, is to transplant into these empty abstractions that personal moral spirit, the defender of custom and established right, which is being driven out of the concrete world by the development of the scientific view. His task is to preserve animism at all costs, and to show that the " highest " function of the mind after all, and no matter what science may achieve, is still to reconcile us with the world, rather than to help us change it.

The history of philosophy shows, of course, a confusing interplay of the two attitudes, the attempt to generalize science, and the metaphysician's art of implanting animism within the assumptions of science. But there is one place in the history of philosophy where the metaphysician's art prevailed absolutely, and became like the Church a national institution, dominating the entire culture of a people, from the public schools to the very laboratories of science. That is modern Germany. German philosophy is the ultimate grandiose convulsion of animistic thought, expiring under the encroachments of the scientific point of view. And the philosophy of Hegel is the ultimate flower of German philosophy, the most adequately bold and all-comprehending and all-obscuring, the most sublimely animistic and the most beautiful. Moreover it is the most dexterous. Declaring that the specific motion of your mind, guided by Hegel, among the logical categories, is the universal self-active motion of those categories, and that this motion is the spirit of God in a process of self-contradiction and development, Hegel succeeded in converting logic itself, the very technique of science, into theology. And having put living movement into the divine abstractions contemplated by this logic-theology, he was able to declare that the material world and all the science which investigates it, are a mere manifestation of these divine abstractions, and yet at the same time assert that this material world is a perpetual process of change and development. This was just what the natural scientists of his time were beginning to believe about the world, and for that reason Hegel's philosophy had an enormous vogue. It entrenched animism in the very heart and centre of the advance that was made by science in the nineteenth century. It made of that science itself and of the mechanically evolving world which it revealed, a church in which God lived, and in which, in spite of its hard-seeming and cruel ways, God was but realizing Himself by His characteristic process of conflicting with Himself, and then resolving the conflict in a higher unity. In short, it declared the essence of reality to be akin to the aspirations of pious men, and hard at work upon the task of realizing them. It preached a gallant and obedient participation in the process.

" The true reason-world, so far from being the exclusive property of philosophy, is the right of every human being on whatever grade of culture or mental growth he may stand.

. . . Man above all things becomes aware of the reasonable order, when he knows of God, and knows Him to be the completely self-determined. Similarly the consciousness a citizen has of his country and its laws is a perception of the reason-world, so long as he looks up to them as unconditioned and likewise universal powers, to which he must subject his individual will. And in the same sense, the knowledge and will of the child is rational when he knows his parents will, and wills it."

That was the moral, and the essential meaning, of the Hegelian " Speculative Logic ".

To people of revolutionary temperament, however, this wholesale doctrine of change offered an equally fine opportunity to rationalize *their* aspirations. There was no inherent reason, it seemed, why this divine Thinking-Process should be so pious and tiresome. If it really likes conflict and change, why won't It give Its sanction to the rebels, to whose who really want conflict right now, and would like to see one more " higher unity " before they die ? That was the mood of the " Young Hegelians ", and among them Marx and Engels. Marx's childhood was less churchly-religious than that of Engels, but their educations were similar, and they approached the world in young manhood with the same mystic emotion. At the age of twenty-three, in dedicating a " Doctor's Thesis " to his future father-in-law, Marx wrote as follows :

" Would that all who doubt of the Idea might be as fortunate as I, to admire an ever-young old man, who greets each advance of time with the enthusiasm and poise of the Truth, and with that conviction-deep, sun-clear Idealism, which alone knows the right word to call up all the spirits of the world, who never recoils before the shadows of reactionary spectres, before the oft-overclouded sky of the times, but with godlike energy and manly sure glance pierces always through all metamorphoses to the empyrean which burns in the heart of the world. You, my fatherly friend, have always been to me a living *argumentum ad oculos*, that Idealism is not a fancy, but a truth.

" Upon you I need not call down a bodily blessing. Spirit is the great magical physician in whom you have put your trust."

And at the age of twenty-two Engels wrote as follows :

" And that faith in the omnipotence of the Idea, in the victory of eternal truth, that firm certainty that it will never waver, never depart from its path, although the whole world turn against it—there you have the foundation of the real positive philosophy, the philosophy of universal history. Just that is the supreme revelation, the revelation of man to man, in which every negation of the critic becomes an affirmation. That everlasting struggle and movement of peoples and heroes, above which in the eternal world soars the Idea, only to swoop down into the thick of the fight and become the actual, self-conscious soul—there you have the source of every salvation and redemption, there the kingdom in which everyone of us ought to struggle and be active at his post. . . ."

In this perfectly animistic attitude Marx and Engels developed their intellectual powers, and formed their habits of thought. Their thinking consisted, up to the age of about twenty-five and twenty-three respectively, in imputing their aspirations to the Ultimate Spirit of the world, and then proceeding fervently to co-operate with that Spirit. And this animistic habit—so native to all human minds—became too strong upon them ever to be overcome. Marx was beginning to sense the harsh character of the contemporary struggle, when Ludwig Feuerbach's writings came into his hands ; he must have felt already the unfitness of the Hegelian " Idea " to preside in such a struggle. And that is doubtless a reason why he welcomed Feuerbach's writings with such enthusiasm. Declaring joyfully that there is no Idea, no " empyrean which burns in the heart of the world " —that the ultimate reality is not spirit, but matter—he went forward from that point without sentimental or confused emotion, and in what seemed an entirely matter-of-fact temper to write the science of proletarian revolution.

But in spite of the great emotional change that had taken place in him, his writings were still metaphysical, still in essence animistic. He did not examine this material world, as an artisan examines the materials of his trade, in order to determine by what means he could make something else out of it. He examined it as the priest examines the ideal world, in order to see if he could not find in it, or failing that, transplant into it his own creative aspiration. Marxism in its intellectual form was not a step from utopian to scientific socialism—; from impractical evangelical talk about a better society, to a practical plan, based upon a study of the existing society, for producing a better one. Marxism was a step from utopian socialism to a socialist religion—a scheme for convincing the believer that the universe itself is producing a better society, and that he has only to fall in properly with the general movement of this universe.

" We explained," says Marx, in describing his own inno- vation, " that it is not a question of putting through some utopian system, but of taking a conscious part in the process of social transformation which is going on before our very eyes."

That was Marx's conception of a scientific under- taking. And that explains his dissatisfaction with Feuerbach's philosophy, his going back to Hegel to get the " dynamic principle " which he missed in the new

material world. It was not merely motion that he
missed, nor a particular kind of motion, but motion in
a congenial direction. He wanted a world which contained his desires and would co-operate with him—a
world in which " by means of all seeming accidents,
and in spite of all momentary set-backs, there is carried
out in the end a progressive development ", " an endless
ascending from the lower to the higher ". It was not
because of emotional dependence, I believe, but because
of his intellectual habits. Marx had the " dynamic
principle " in his own will, but being a German philosopher, he had not the least idea that true science, like
simple practical thought, might consist of defining a purpose and compelling the external world into its service.

Thus when Marx said in his " Theses on Feuerbach "
that sensation is a practical activity, he did not mean
that sensation is an instrument for solving the problems
of the sentient being. He meant that it is an instrument
for solving problems common to the sentient being and
the world that produced him. His fundamental statement in that first thesis was not that sensation is a practical activity, but that the sensible *object* is to be
understood *subjectively*. And his fundamental statement
in the whole of those comments on Feuerbach was this :
" The simultaneous occurrence of a change of circumstances and of human activity or *self-change*, can only
be comprehended and rationally understood as *revolutionary practice*." That shows what Marx meant by
the word " Praxis ", and it shows the direction in which
his mind was travelling. He was not advancing from
Feuerbach's philosophy toward the modern science of
thought as an instrument for getting along in a material
and social world. He was shrinking back from Feuerbach into the more familiar Hegelian position, in which
true thought and the material world are doing the same

thing, and doing it together. That statement about the simultaneous occurrence of a change of circumstances and " self-change ", fulfils much the same function in the animism of Marx, that is fulfilled in Christian animism by the statement, " God helps them who help themselves ".

Plekhanov has a passage in which he describes the mental process by which Marx became a " scientific socialist ". And it is valuable, not only as stating the animistic attitude of Marx, but as indicating how perfectly that attitude was preserved in Plekhanov himself, the founder of Russian Marxism.

" A disciple of Hegel," he says, " remaining true to the method of his teacher, could become a socialist only in case a scientific investigation of the contemporary economic structure brought him to the conclusion that its inner lawful development leads to the birth of the socialist order."

In other words, if you wish to create a socialist order, there is only one way to go about it, and that is to persuade yourself that the inner law of the objective world is creating it for you. If this attitude is remote from prayer, it is remote in the direction of its primitive origins. Dialectic Materialism rests its hope in the very sticks and stones, instead of in a spirit that is supposed to reside behind them. Otherwise it is not different from any other animistic philosophy. And whatever may have been the case with Marx, it is certain that many of his followers derive from this philosophy a support not unlike that derived by the pious from their God.

" If in spite of all the violence of its enemies," writes Rosa Luxemburg, " the contemporary workers' movement marches triumphantly forward with its head high, that is due above all to its tranquil understanding of the ordered objective historic development, its understanding of the fact that ' capitalist production creates with the necessity of a natural process its own negation—namely, the expropriation of the expropriators, the socialist revolution '. In this understanding the workers' movement sees the firm guarantee of its ultimate victory, and from this source it derives not only its zeal, but its patience, not only strength for action, but also courageous restraint and endurance."

It is not difficult to recognize in those lines the essential features of a religious psychology.

In answering those who asked the Marxians why, if socialism is the necessary product of economic evolution, they struggle to attain it, Plekhanov cited the struggle of the Puritans, the Mahometans, Calvin's Moses labouring to achieve what was predetermined by God, and the great Cromwell who always named his acts the fruit of the Divine Will.

" Here all depends," said Plekhanov, " on the question whether my own activity constitutes a necessary link in the chain of necessary events. If yes—then so much the less do I waver, so much the more decisively I act."

Plekhanov was perfectly right in relating the animistic materialism of Marx to the faith of the prophets. And he was right also in asserting that animistic faith does not put a stop to practical efforts. History would read very differently if it did. But he was wrong in thinking that it makes any difference to " me " whether I conceive my practical activity as a necessary link in the necessary process or not. That makes a difference only to the philosopher who talks about me. And it makes a difference to him, because his job is to reconcile animism with the *theoretic assumptions* of my practical activity.

And fatalism, or the idea that the result of these activities is going to be regulated externally, is too obviously in conflict with those assumptions. Therefore he must take the idea of *causal determination*, which is one of those assumptions, and by some sort of intellectual hocus-pocus he must give it the upper hand over the idea of a *genuine alternative* in thought and action, which is another. And thus he may preserve animism for a while as a philosophy, even after it has ceased as a religion to impose upon my practical mind.

The definition of freedom as *necessity become conscious*, was invented by German philosophers for this express purpose. It was invented by Schelling, but greatly improved in the way of unintelligibility by Hegel, who mixed it up with his myth about everything becoming its opposite, and contrived to make his reader feel at times as though a person does really become creative when he becomes conscious. In the end, however, it appears that it is only because the cause which determines him, is also *him*, that *he* ceases, or seems to cease, to be determined when he becomes aware of the truth. Freedom is " the truth of necessity ", according to Hegel. And the real significance of this statement is revealed in his philosophy of religion, when he says that a man is free when he " wants nothing but himself ". He is free, that is, when he wants nothing which would involve a change in the conditions which produced him.

Marx accepted this dictum of Hegel's uncritically, and Plekhanov declared the original statement of Schelling to be " one of the most brilliant discoveries ever made by philosophic thought ". Here again Plekhanov is entirely right, but it is necessary to remember just what philosophic thought is, and what its purpose is. The conception of the entire evolving variety of the world as held in the frame of an iron necessity, is not an essential part of the attempt to generalize science. The laws of science are an abstraction from the variety of nature, and that variety itself bears witness that these laws are not, and cannot be, an adequate or absolute statement of nature. The law of causation is not different from any other of these scientific laws. Moreover the very existence of science and its development, can be explained only upon the assumption that thought has a function other than the mere reflection or transmission of an already defined impulse. It has the function of defining impulse. That the future is in some degree undetermined is therefore the ineradicable assumption of all thinking. And this is nowhere more evident than in the thinking of Plekhanov about the doctrine of necessity. For his whole argument is this : *if I should cease to make efforts*, because I believe in that doctrine, I would be unreasonable. And that hypothetical proposition, *if I should*, implies a genuine alternative. It is only our acceptance of the genuineness of that alternative, that gives intelligibility to those long pages of Plekhanov and makes it possible to read or think them. And that hypothetical proposition *if I should*, is moreover the original, and in a sense also the universal, form of all thinking.

When Engels says that " Freedom does not consist in a fancied independence of the laws of nature, but in the knowledge of those laws and the possibility thereby created of deliberately making them function toward defined ends ", he shows either a naïve innocence of the problem he is talking about, or that Hegelian sophistication which is a mockery of innocence. For the fact that my thinking which assumes to define ends in the future, operates with causal laws which assume that the future is already defined, is exactly the essence of the problem. The most advanced science, like the most simple practical sagacity, insists upon the validity of both those assumptions. It insists that there are, on the one hand, an adequate number of general and reliable uniformities in nature, and that there is, on the other hand, a genuine alternative in thought and action—a possibility that " I may ", or " may not ". These two assumptions are not absolutely contradictory, and if there is a profound mental difficulty in reconciling them, it is in the spirit of science—and especially of science as humbled by the understanding of its own origin—to leave that difficulty standing until a real solution is found. The demand that one should take his stand with Absolute Determinism and the impossibility of explaining what thought is and how it arose, or with Absolute Caprice and the impossibility of effective thinking, is a demand that comes, like other " absolute " demands, from the metaphysical and not the scientific mind. Its purpose is just the purpose of all metaphysics—to preserve the sovereignty of the Divine Spirit in spite of the advance of the practical arts.

Marx not only failed to escape from philosophy with his dialectic materialism, but he failed to escape, in the essence of the matter, from idealistic philosophy. For if your material world has the faculty of willing the social revolution, and aspiring toward all those good things grouped by a revolutionary mind under the concept of " higher ", and if it has the faculty of going after those things by a procedure that is in its essence logical, what is there left of mind that you have not surreptitiously attributed to this material world ? There is left feeling only—if the attributes of mind are " will and thought and feeling "—and it was exactly and only a feeling that Marx got rid of, when he turned from Hegelian idealism to a materialism that was also Hegelian.

He got rid of the ethico-deific feeling which idealistic philosophers attribute to the ultimate reality, and which makes their sense of co-operation with it sentimental and humble and conservative. Marx's ultimate reality is ascending " from the lower to the higher " cold-bloodedly and without caring anything about it. And that leaves him free, while co-operating with that reality, to have irreverent emotions, and be as hard-headed and ruthless as it is necessary for a practical revolutionist to be.

That is the extent of the " materialism " of Marx. And that explains why Marx and Engels repudiated with such violence " the materialism of natural science ", " the materialism which exists to-day in the minds of naturalists and physicians ", calling it " abstract ", and " mechanical " and even " shallow and vulgar ". Why should one kind of materialism describe another kind as shallow and vulgar ? Whence indeed this word vulgar on the lips of a revolutionist ? It is the Marxian way of saying *profane*. Marx and Engels were defending against scientific materialism—against that attitude which constitutes the simple common-sense starting-point of science—a materialistic religion.

And that explains, too, another thing which has troubled many critical minds attempting to enter into the Marxian system. It explains why Marx and Engels thought they could call their economic explanation of history a " materialistic " explanation. There is not the slightest logical connection between materialistic *philosophy* and the economic interpretation of history. One could believe that the course of history is entirely determined by wagging tongues, and still be a materialistic philosopher. And one could believe that it is all a matter of the instruments of production, and still believe that those instruments, like everything else, are in their ultimate reality ideas. Marx drove out of the study of history the same *feeling* that he drove out of Hegel's philosophy. That is the only connection between dialectic materialism and the economic interpretation of history. It was a matter-of-fact interpretation of history, and it is a matter-of-fact philosophy—so far as one can be matter-of-fact, and still retain that animistic attitude which is the essence of philosophy.

The purposive thought which explains Marx's intellectual position, is contained in these sentences written in his early youth :

" The abolition of religion, the illusory happiness of the people, is a demand for their real happiness. The demand that one reject illusions about one's situation, is a demand that one reject a situation which has need of illusions."

That rejection of illusions—religious, moralistic, legal, political, æsthetic—is the immortal essence of Marx's contribution to the science of history, and to history itself. And if he did not succeed in rejecting also the illusions of philosophy, those who really esteem his life and his genius ought to carry out the process. Marx himself declared that philosophy, like law and politics and religion, and art, is subject to an economic interpretation at the hands of science. But he also declared —and within a year of the same date—that Hegel wrote the true history of philosophy. Since Hegel's history of philosophy is a history of " the self-developing reason ", a " history of thought finding itself ", these two statements are directly contradictory, and we have to choose between them. We have to choose between Marxism as a Hegelian philosophy, and Marxism as a science which is capable of explaining such philosophy.

CHAPTER IV

THE MARXIAN INTERPRETATION OF HISTORY

HEGEL regarded history as the logical evolution of the Eternal Thinking Process in a disguised form. It was a process of advance by contradiction and the negation of the negation. And his philosophy of history consisted in seeking out in the " everlasting struggle of peoples and heroes " this necessary dialectic development, which was the one real cause and explanation of the course of that struggle, no matter what those who took part in it might be thinking or intending. Marx retained the principal assumptions of this philosophy : namely, that history is some one thing or process, irrespective of the interests of a given historian ; that this process has some one cause, other than the conscious purposes of men, which explains it all ; and that this cause has the property of being logical in its development, and of advancing by contradiction, and the negation of the negation. He retained this much of the Hegelian philosophy of history, but he turned that philosophy other side up. He found the ultimate one cause, not in the evolving Idea, which " soars above history in the eternal world ", but in the evolving forces of production which lie underneath the soaring eloquence of history as it is usually written.

" In the social production of their subsistence men enter into determined and necessary relations with each other which are independent of their wills—production-relations which correspond to a definite stage of development of their material productive forces. The sum of these production-relations forms the economic structure of society, the real basis upon which a juridical and political superstructure arises, and to which definite social forms of consciousness correspond. The mode of production of the material subsistence, conditions the social, political and spiritual life-process in general. It is not the consciousness of men which determines their existence, but on the contrary it is their social existence which determines their consciousness. At a certain stage of their development the material productive forces of society come into contradiction with the existing production-relations, or what is merely a juridical expression for the same thing, the property relations within which they have operated before. From being forms of development of the productive forces, these relations turn into fetters upon their development. Then comes an epoch of social revolution. With the change in the economic foundation the whole immense superstructure is slowly or rapidly transformed. In studying such a transformation one must always distinguish between the material transformation in the economic conditions essential to production—which can be established with the exactitude of natural science—and the juridical, political, religious, artistic, or philosophic, in short ideological forms, in which men become conscious of this conflict and fight it out. As little as one judges what an individual is by what he thinks of himself, so little can one judge such an epoch of transformation by its consciousness ; one must rather explain this consciousness by the contradictions in the material life, the conflict at hand between the social forces of production and the relations in which production is carried on. No social formation ever disappears before all the productive forces are developed for which it has room, and new higher relations of production never appear before the material conditions of their existence are matured in the womb of the old society."

In those sentences you can see all three of the Hegelian presuppositions I spoke of. You see that the whole historic life of society, and humanity in it, is regarded as one single thing or movement ; that it has one general cause of which men are not conscious ; and that this cause operates by a process of logical contradiction. The " productive forces " come into contradiction with the " production-relations ", and this contradiction, resolving itself in a higher unity, constitutes the underlying cause of the whole movement. To a concrete or very realistic mind, the idea of a " contradiction " between forces and relations, is so abstract and undynamic as to be incapable of explaining any motion whatever. And such minds usually pass this over as merely an example of Marx's peculiar way of talking. This peculiar way of talking belongs to the essence of Marx's thought. He is not trying to explain history dynamically, but logically—or rather, with a mixture of dynamics and logic in which logic will invariably have the last word. He is seeking, not only underneath the ideologies of men for their class-struggles, but also underneath their class-struggles for an antithesis between two " concrete universals ", whose resolution according to the principles of the Hegelian logic will necessitate the victory of the lower class. That is why he describes a social revolution as a " contradiction " between two generalities. And that is why he forgets sometimes this key-word " contradiction " and speaks of it as a conflict, or even a " rebellion " of one generality against another. " The forces of production rebell against the mode of production which they have outgrown." And the mystic perfection with which this state of affairs arises and moves to its conclusion may be seen in the dictum that " No social formation ever disappears until all the productive forces are developed for which it has room ". Obviously the mere dynamics of a concrete conflict could never give us this admirable assurance. What we have to do with here is not dynamics, but " Speculative Logic ".

There is really no foundation in fact for any of the three assumptions which Marx borrowed from Hegel. History is no one thing or process, except as it is made so by the interests of the historian ; it has no one cause, either within or without the consciousness of men, which explains it all ; it does not advance by a process of dialectic contradiction and the negation of the negation. Hence it has been necessary for Marxians to qualify this concise and brilliant metaphysical statement in various practical ways. One of these ways was indicated by Marx himself in the third and fourth sentences, where he interchanges the verbs *condition* and *determine* as though they were approximately equivalent. It is obvious that if the material basis positively *determined* the superstructure, we should not have to disregard the superstructure and examine the basis, for the one could be directly inferred from the other. Thus the control exercised by the economic factor turns out to be in the nature of the case merely negative. And the followers of Marx, without exactly noticing this, have been content if they could show in the case of any particular historic development that economic factors *had something essential to do with it*. Lafargue, for instance, points out that if there had *not* been " systematic, rational stock-breeding " in England, Darwin could not have invented his theory of evolution. This is far, of course, from saying that economic forces caused, or determined, or " in the last analysis explain " the theory of evolution. And it is something that might be more easily proven by pointing out that if Darwin had not had anything to eat, he could not have invented the theory of evolution. Marxians defend their philosophy of history by darting back and forth between a truism and a quite fantastic assertion, and never getting caught in either the one position or the other. It is a familiar method in metaphysics, but it has nothing to do with science. A theory which ignores the difference between the verbs *condition* and *determine* cannot be called scientific, because it has not sufficient exactitude to be verified.

There are two other ideas which Marxians interchange without noticing it. At one time they present the political and cultural superstructure as a *result* of economic causes, at another time as a *reflection* of economic conditions. The Marxian explanation of law and the state, for example, may be and usually is expressed in a causal form. The development of the forces of production brings classes into conflict, and the exploiting class in order to preserve its supremacy, creates or appropriates the state, and codifies those customs and those moral ideas and tendencies which are favourable to its supremacy. This state and these ideas and tendencies are not " reflections " of the economic process ; they are nothing like it. They are results of it, and the process of their creation can be analysed causally and scientifically understood. But when you pass into spheres which are farther away from the economic basis— religion, for instance, or art, which is half play, and therefore least of all subject to a business explanation —Marxians abandon all pretence at causal analysis, and merely assert that these things are an automatic symbolic picture of the economic conditions.

Marx dismisses the whole problem of the psychology of religion with the statement that " the religious world is merely a reflection of the real world ". And Engels furnishes an example : Calvin's doctrine of predestination, was the " religious expression of the fact that in the commercial world of competition success or failure does not depend upon a man's activity or cleverness, but upon circumstances uncontrolled by him ". That is an interesting remark, but if you approach the doctrine of Calvin from the point of view of real causation—as Engels does, indeed, in another book—you get an opposite result. Religion is within the control of the ruling classes, and their one concern in a commercial world of competition is to keep the people convinced that their success or failure *does* depend upon their activity and cleverness. If Marxism were a science of history, it would long ago have cleared up this elementary confusion. As a philosophy of history it is vitally concerned to preserve it.

Trotsky explains futurism as a " reflection in art " of the " unheard-of industrial boom " of the last twenty years, " which overthrew old ideas of wealth and power, worked out new scales, new criteria of the possible and the impossible ". That also is an interesting literary remark, but it is not a scientific explanation. How far it is from science, may be seen in the observation with which Trotsky is compelled to supplement it :

" We have observed the following phenomenon, repeated more than once in history : that backward countries, which nevertheless possess a certain level of spiritual culture, reflect more clearly and more strongly in their ideology the attainments of advanced countries. Thus German thought in the eighteenth and nineteenth centuries reflected the economic achievements of the English. . . . Futurism received its clearest expression, not in America, not in Germany, but in Italy and Russia."

No mind trained in the investigation of concrete causes, trained in their accurate definition and verification, could possibly rest in this statement. By what material connection does the economic development of England produce its strongest reflection in Germany, and that of America, in Russia ? And how does it happen that this reflection does not arise in Australia, or for that matter in the Polar Sea ?

In order really to explain futurist art upon the basis of an economic boom, you would have to show that actual artists, or the artist class, were in a position where in order to get a good share of the benefits of that boom, they were led to make pictures and write poems that were a " reflection " of it. And you would find it more easy to prove the opposite thesis. What artists are best paid for during an industrial boom, is keeping the idle thoughts of the public occupied with Eternal Beauty, holding fast to the old ideas of wealth and power, and giving no unnecessary impetus to " new criteria of the possible and the impossible ". Nevertheless, because of the mystic emotion attached by Marxists to the word economic, and because of the complete absence in Marxism of the mere conception of a psychological science, this remark of Trotsky's is accepted by his followers as precisely what it is not, an *analytical* discussion of the causes of futurist art. And artists who read it, instead of seeing their unconscious motives explained, and profiting to the extent of their intelligence by the explanation, see themselves abstractly and mystically dominated by a strange new Deity with a scientific name. And they learn that whatever their self-knowledge may be, and whatever their effort, the work they produce can turn out nothing in the long run but an automatic image of the face of this Deity, the Economic Basis of the society in which they live. That is poison to art, but it is one of the essential ways in which Hegelian Marxians preserve their metaphysical dogma in face of the irreducible variety of the world.

Another way, and a far more promising one, if they could be held to it, is to declare that Economic Deter-

minism is only a " principle of investigation ". It is
difficult to understand how anybody could make this
statement, as orthodox Marxians very often do, and
at the same time assert that economic determinism is
an ultimate and irrefutable philosophy of history. The
explanation lies in a fact already mentioned, and which
the reader of this book must bear continually in mind
—namely, that Marxism is not pure and natural metaphysics. Marxism is a seventy-five years' struggle
between metaphysics and an instinctive practical-
scientific realism, in which metaphysics carried the day.
A critic is compelled to do some violence to the practically
realistic side of this struggle. He is compelled to set
Marxism back clearly and definitely into that metaphysical frame from which it did not in the long run
escape. The idea that economic determinism is merely
a " principle of investigation ", was one of the momentary
victories of practical science.

Another slight but highly important exception to
economic determinism has to be made by all orthodox
Marxians. They all have to assert that although Germany
in the period of her " classical philosophy " was in a
very backward economic phase, and although her political state corresponded accurately to her economic
development—being, in the words of Engels, a " feudal
and bureaucratic despotism "—and although her classical
philosophers were " instructors of youth appointed by
the state "—nevertheless the speculations of these
classical philosophers were the most advanced achievement of the scientific mind up to that date, and " behind
their pedantically obscure utterances, and in their heavy
wearisome periods . . . the revolution lay concealed ".
The fact is that these classical German philosophers
were just as backward as the state which employed

them, and they were backward in the same way. The German state patronized modern capitalism, perverting it to the support of feudal political institutions ; and the German philosophers patronized modern science, perverting it to the support of animistic superstition. The revolution, far from " lying concealed " in the alien and astutely reactionary speculations of these philosophers, and issuing legitimately from them, lay concealed in ideas and impulses quite apart from anything known by these philosophers. But in the process of its birth it got tangled up in their speculations, and well-nigh buried and choked to death there, and it has never completely issued from them at all, but carries along on its back a burden of " pedantically obscure utterances and heavy wearisome periods " that bear witness to its origin in a country which had not reached an advanced stage of economic development. If Marxians would apply their principle of economic determinism to the German classical philosophy, they would be relieved of the necessity of applying it to everything else under the sun. For they would see that *as a principle of universal application*, it is nothing but a relic of the attempt of " instructors of youth appointed by the state " in an ceonomically backward country, to prevent the youth of that country from falling into the scepticism of modern science.

Another small loop-hole in economic determinism was discovered by Plekhanov, who pointed out, somewhat timidly, that a man who understands Marxism may by that very fact be enabled to exercise a little special influence upon history.

" If I know," says Plekhanov, " in what direction the social relations are changing, thanks to given changes in the social process of production, then I know also in what direction the social mind is going to change. Consequently I have a chance to influence it. To influence the social mind means to influence the historic event. Thus in a certain sense, I may even make history, and not just wait for it to make itself."

It did not occur to Plekhanov that a man who understands economic determinism might change history by attacking the economic basis directly, as Lenin did when he undertook to communize Russia by means of electrification. Plekhanov approached those evolving " social relations " created by the forces of production as one approaches a living God. " The character of a personality," he exclaimed, " is a factor in social development only where, only when, and only in so far as, social relations permit it ! " An exclamation which means nothing at all, unless " social relations " are personified, and the word *permit* taken to mean " give permission ". Otherwise it is equally true that social relations can be a factor in development only when, only where, and only in so far as, the character of personalities permits it. And indeed they both can be factors, only in so far as cabbages or cows permit it.

In addition to these unrecognized or unofficial ways of modifying the rigour of economic determinism, there is the official Hegelian way indicated by Marx himself— the appeal to the principle of Accident.

" World history would indeed be easy to make," said Marx, " if the struggle were always engaged only on condition of indubitably favourable chances. Nature moreover would be very mystical if ' accidents ' played no rôle. These accidents fall quite naturally into the general course of the development, and are compensated for by other accidents. But acceleration and retardation are very dependent upon such ' accidents ' among which figures such an ' accident ' as the characters of the people who stand first at the head of a movement."

The reader will notice that Marx sometimes puts the word " accident " in quotation marks, but sometimes not. And this is an accurate indication of his state of mind about the problem involved. The same state of mind is indicated in Engels' use of the phrase " accidents or seeming accidents ". It is a correctly Hegelian state of mind. Hegel conceived of chance, not as a mere name for our ignorance of causes, but as a genuine objective element in nature's evolution. It was only *underneath*, and *through*, and *in spite of*, chance events— events which " may or may not be "—that Hegel's divine necessity was to be found working its way to the inevitable goal. And yet at the same time Hegel believed that most apparent accidents can be proven to have been inevitable, and should be so proven by the philosophic mind.

" The problem of science," he said, " and especially of philosophy, undoubtedly consists in eliciting the necessity concealed under the semblance of contingency. That however is far from meaning that the contingent belongs to our subjective conception alone, and must therefore be simply set aside, if we wish to get at the truth. All scientific researches which pursue this course exclusively, lay themselves fairly open to the charge of mere jugglery and an over-strained precisianism."

It is this opinion of Hegel which reappears in Marx's statement that accidents fall " quite naturally " into the general course of development, but are—*quite supernaturally*, we cannot refrain from saying—compensated for by other accidents of an opposite kind. Not only the " materialism " of Marx is not materialistic, but his determinism is not the determinism of mechanical science. The ultimate historic event is necessary, according to Marx, not because all events are bound togethoger by perfect chain of causes, but because through a whole sea of chance happenings—some really accidental, and some only seeming so to our ignorance —the " inner laws " of history are working to their inevitable ends. The essential animism of this conception is clearly apparent in the writings of Engels, who always speaks of history as being " governed " by these mysterious laws.

" Historical events appear to be wholly controlled by chance. But even where on the surface accident plays its part, it is always governed by inner, hidden laws."

That this whole doctrine is animistic metaphysics, becomes most obvious when Marxians discuss the rôle of their own heroes in history. This is one of the problems which trouble them the most, for having a really great hero—and two, indeed, since Lenin lived and died—they are naturally great hero-worshippers. And yet their philosophy seems to deny the essential value of heroes. Engels says that " If there had been no Napoleon, another would have taken his place ", and he makes almost the same assertion about Karl Marx. He makes it a little less glibly, however, and most Marxians have sought to avoid the extreme stoicism of such a statement. They have sought to avoid also, I suppose, its extreme foolishness. For if there exists any point in all the egregious intellectual chatter of Simian man when it behooves him to say " I do not know ", it is when such questions arise as " What would have happened if there had been no Napoleon ? " " What would have happened if there had been no Marx ? "

The orthodox way to reconcile the historic importance of Marx with the tenets of his own philosophy, is that indicated in the passage which I quoted about " accidents ". The leaders of a movement cannot alter the direction or outcome of the historical process, but they can alter its speed. Trotsky tries always to be orthodox, although he is a little impatient of his orthodoxy, and here is what Trotsky says :

" Of course, of course, of course, we know that the working class will triumph. We sing ' No man will deliver us ' and we add ' No hero '. And that is true, but only in the last historical account. That is, in the last account of history the working class would have conquered if there had never been a Marx in the world, if there had never been a Lenin. The working class would work out those ideas which are needful to it, those methods which are needful to it, but more slowly. The circumstance that the working class on the two crests of its flood has raised up two such figures as Marx and Lenin, is a gigantic advantage to the revolution."

That is the fundamental Marxian position. But it is subject to a further slight modification in the direction of common sense and human sentiment. For upon reflection it appears that if these rather rambunctious accidents, such as Marx and Lenin, can alter the speed of the historic process, they do really play an enormous rôle in determining the character of history. In a world in which " everything flows ", to hasten or to delay an event is to alter it. Thus it must be assumed that when Trotsky says " in the last historical account "—and this phrase he brings directly from Engels—he means that, although the ultimate result considered abstractly is economically determined, these non-economically determined accidents can alter the concrete details of the procedure by which we get to it. They can not only make the path longer or shorter, but they can make it more or less " thorny ", as Kautsky says. Or as he formulates it more precisely : Although they cannot influence " the direction of the development ", they can influence " its course, and the road by which it arrives at the inevitable result ". Is it not obvious, however, that if the historic road is different, then the result also. *taken concretely*, will be different ?

Indeed, in that very word " result ", the animistic personification of " history ", which lies at the bottom of this whole theory, is unmistakably revealed. History considered concretely and objectively and without projecting into it the emotional interests of the historian, contains no " results ". History is just a series or congeries of events, or at the best a " process ", and the road travelled is all there is of it. If the economic factor merely determines certain points on this road—whether a given historian chooses to call those points " results " or not, the objective question remains, just which points they are, and how many. And that is exactly the manner in which the question is posed by those who reject economic determinism in its orthodox form, but yet " recognize the value of the idea "—Bernstein, Jaurès, Benedetto Croce, Simkhovitch, Professor Seligman— those whom orthodox Marxians despise with a kind of fear, because they insist on introducing degree into the economic determination, and asking the scientific question " How much ? " The orthodox Marxians really differ from them, not in refusing to admit that history is only *in some degree* determined economically, but in personifying history, and imputing to it a goal, or a " result ", or a series of " results ", and declaring that *these* are determined economically. They are defending an abstract animistic philosophy of history against a concrete scientific study of historic events.

This is nowhere more apparent than in the famous letters about economic determinism written by Engels long after the death of Marx. In these letters Engels introduced such sweeping concrete qualifications and exceptions in detail to the control exercised by the economic factor in history, that it seemed possible to

Bernstein to declare that Engels had surrendered the essence of the Marxian theory. But at the same time Engels re-asserted the ultimate and abstract control exercised by the economic factor in its most Hegelian purity, and thus enabled Kautsky to reply that he had surrendered nothing at all.

" The economic situation is the basis," wrote Engels, " but the various elements of the superstructure, the political forms of the class-struggle and its results, the system of government established by the victorious class after the battle, etc., legal forms, even the reflection of all these real conflicts in the brain of the participants, political, juridical, and philosophic theories, religious outlooks and their further development into dogmatic systems, exercise their influence upon the course of the historic struggle, and in many cases predominantly determine its forms. . . ."

And again :

" The low economic development of the prehistoric period had as its compliment, and at times even as its condition and even as its cause, false representations of nature. . . . It would be pedantry to seek economic causes for all these elementary stupidities. The history of science is the history of the gradual elimination of this nonsense, or its replacement by other nonsense a little less absurd. The people who do this belong to a special sphere of the division of labour, and it seems that they are developing an independent realm. And in so far as they form a self-dependent group within the social division of labour, so far their productions, including their mistakes, *exercise a retro-active influence* upon the whole social development, even the economic."

Thus Engels went out of his way to explain that a body of ideas for whose origin it would be " absurd " to seek economic causes, and which may indeed have been itself the cause of economic processes, does nevertheless in the course of its career influence the whole social development. This seems far away, indeed, from the original drastic statement of the Marxian philosophy of history. And yet Engels has sacrificed nothing of the essence of that philosophy. Its whole heart and purpose is satisfied when he declares, in strictly Hegelian language :

The historic process " is a reciprocal action of all these factors upon each other, wherein ultimately through all the infinite number of accidents (things and events, the inner connections of which are so remote and undemonstrable, that we may count them as non-existent and ignore them), the economic movement in the form of necessity is carried through."

Economic determinism was in its origin just as mystical and mysterious, and disposed to ignore an infinite number of things which it could not explain, as it is in this final formulation. It was simply the pious metaphysical assertion of Hegel that " Spirit is the only moving principle in history ", turned into the impious, but equally metaphysical assertion that the forces of production are the only moving principle in history—the only " changing element ", as Kautsky explicitly puts it. Neither of these absolute statements has any basis in fact or probability. And the whole half-century's discussion, so exasperating to reason, so fiuitless, so destructive of all naïvely-clear thinking, has value simply as a picture of the highest revolutionary intelligence trying unsuccessfully to escape from the bonds of German metaphysics.

There is only one way to escape from those bonds. That is to take the revolutionary motive back out of " history ", where Marx and Engels surreptitiously projected it, and locate it in the human breast where it belongs. It was Marx and not History, that was deter-

mined to produce a social revolution, and his investigation
of history was an attempt to find out the method by
which it could be done.   When that simple truth—as
obvious to a child as it is inaccessible to a Marxian—
has once been acknowledged, the whole discussion loses
its mystifying character at once.   History is relieved
of the strait-jacket of a statement wholly inadequate
to express its variety, and the Marxian is relieved of the
necessity of proving something that, even if it were
true, is beyond the capacity of human science to prove.
He has no longer any fear of a quantitative statement of
the control exercised by the economic factor upon social
evolution, because he is able to state clearly what quantity
of control he believes to be exercised by that factor.   It
is a control sufficient to render impractical and ineffectual
any attempt to revolutionize society, in the direction
contemplated by socialists or anarchists or early Christians,
by means of operations directed against, or conducted
within, the political and ideological superstructure.   It
is a negative control ; economic determinism is like the
demon of Socrates, it tells you only what you cannot
do.   But at the same time it is a dynamic control, whose
operation can be analysed and demonstrated in detail,
and not a kind of mystic correspondence entirely incapable of verification.   Its recognition is not a " philosophy of history ", and it requires no patching up with
special appeals to the principle of accident ;   no explaining away and explaining back again of the greatness
of great men ; no imputation to history of a personal
interest in results ; no concealing under mountains of
pretentiously disinterested and abstract talk the particular
results in which Marxians are interested.   It does not
modestly profess to be a principle of investigation, and
at the same time dogmatically declare itself both a
metaphysical presupposition and a final result of investi-

gations already accomplished. And finally it does not timidly concede that a person who understands it may " in a certain sense ", and in some instances, be enabled by that very fact to " influence an historic event ". It clearly states that the whole cause and purpose of its existence, like that of any other practical science, is to enable the person who understands it to control history to the fullest possible extent.

CHAPTER V

THE THEORY OF CLASS STRUGGLE

For Marx as a philosopher, a class struggle in its " inner " essence was not a concrete fight between people, but an abstract contradiction between generalities—between " forces of production " and " production-relations ". And since all past history was but the dialectic life-story of such contradictions, Marx was able to assert that " All past history, with the exception of its primitive stages, was the history of class-struggles ". What is the truth under this obviously preposterous assertion ?

The word history involves a generalization of the most loose and inclusive sort. It is a name for the whole heterogeneous agglomeration of events and developments which have caught the interest and stuck in the memories of men. The mere fact that history contains a record of the development of every explanation, proves that there can be no single explanation of history. For as soon as you have explained an explanation on the basis of facts other than those contemplated in it, you have destroyed its validity. If the Copernican astronomy is subject to explanation as a result of economic motions on earth, it is not a true science of motion in the heavens. This is but one way of proving that any philosophy of history " penetrated with unity "—any single statement of the essence and essential explanation of the whole past of humanity—belongs itself to that past, which is among other things, let us hope, the grave of metaphysics.

And anyone who proposes such a statement and explanation has already singled out in that past of humanity the particular development which interests him, and it is this which he designates when he uses the word *history*.

The thing that most interested Marx was the effort to create a true human society. The predominating purpose of his life was to find out how to produce, and help to produce, out of the existing social materials, " an association which will exclude classes and their antagonisms, and in which there will no longer be political power properly so called "—a society which " can inscribe on its banner : ' From each according to his abilities, to each according to his needs ! ' " Looking over the pages of history, he observed that ever since the time of primitive communism human society has been in a state of class struggle, open or veiled, and that human relations have never been fundamentally changed in any way except by the victory of a new class in that struggle. Upon the basis of this historic observation, backed up by economics and a hard-headed knowledge of human nature, he was able to assert that the only method by which our existing society can be revolutionized, is the organization of the working-class struggle, and the perfection of its technique. In so far as he was a scientific engineer, and not an animistic philosopher, that is what he did assert. And that is all the truth that any person possessing the mentality of true science, will ever find in the statement, that " the history of all hitherto existing society is the history of class struggles ".

CHAPTER VI

MARX AND DARWIN

MARX greeted Darwin's theory of evolution as a " support from natural science ". And the general Marxian opinion, expressed in numberless articles and pamphlets, is that Darwin's discovery was " a glorious corroboration and completion of the Marxian theory ". Engels said, a little more temperately, that Marx's theory was " destined to do for history what Darwin's theory has done for biology ".

It seems as though Engels' prediction might prove true—although not in the manner he anticipated. For if any one thing is conceded by all biologists to-day, it is that Darwin's theory is not an adequate explanation of the process of organic evolution. Darwin's achievement was to banish the ethico-deific out of biology, establish the fact of evolution upon a scientific basis, and point out a dominating principle of investigation and matter-of-fact explanation. And Marx made almost exactly the same contribution to the general science of history. He put in the place of moralistic and religious and poetic and patriotic eloquences, a matter-of-fact principle of explanation, which has become the dominating one for all freely inquiring minds, and he established —or at least first adequately emphasized—the fact that there has been an evolution, not only in the political forms of society, but in its economic structure.

The differences between Marx and Darwin are just

as significant, however, as their similarities. And the
failure of Marxians to notice them is the chief cause of
the weakness of their present scientific position. Darwin
approached the problem of explaining evolution without
any political purpose or passion. He made no pretence
to foretell the future of the process. His books are a
model of the pure art of inquiry, so far as that art
can be attained by a mind the very forms of whose
thinking are practical. And therefore thev have an
objective validity which Marx could have attained only
if he had recognized the rôle played by his purpose,
and separated that part of his thought which consisted
of analysing facts, from that which consisted of planning
for the realization of an idea.

Darwin also approached his problem of evolution
without any metaphysical presupposition as to the
manner in which evolution proceeds. He was not
afflicted with any " universal law of motion in thought
and in the external world ". Therefore he was entirely
free to let the facts teach him. And they taught him
something quite contrary to that view of thought and
the external world which lies at the bottom of the
Hegelian-Marxian conception of evolution. To Darwin
—or to those who have developed the implications of
his discovery—thinking is not a function belonging
to Nature at large, and evolving mirror-like in friendly
and harmonious parallel with her universal evolution.
Thinking is a function developed by particular organisms
in mortal conflict with other organisms, and with the
inclemency and indifference of Nature at large, and
its character is determined by the requirements of
success in that conflict. Its essence is not to make
pictures of the general environment in the edifying
forms of the philosopher's logic, but to interpret the
important parts of that environment in the practical

forms of nervous and muscular attitude and adaptive action.

Instead of acclaiming Darwin as a mere support and glory of metaphysical Marxism, the thing is to put this ultimate outcome of Darwin's discovery at the bottom of Marxism, in the place of metaphysics.

CHAPTER VII

THE DOCTRINE OF IDEOLOGIES

ONE further exception to the law of economic determinism, more significant than any of those I mentioned, is implied in Marx's own classical statement of it.

In studying revolutions, he says, " one must always distinguish between the material transformation in the economic conditions essential to production—which can be established with the exactitude of natural science—and the juridical, political, religious, artistic or philosophical, in short ideological, forms in which men become conscious of this conflict and fight it out."

In this statement it appears that natural science is not determined by those material changes in the conditions of production which determine the ideological forms of thinking. Natural science is " determined " by those material changes in nature which constitute the object of its study, and by no others. And it appears also that Marxism itself partakes of the independent validity of natural science. In so far as Marxism is a definition of those changes in the conditions of production which are contemporary with it, you may say that it is determined *by* them, and so differs from an ideology only in being conscious of its nature. But in so far as Marxism is " the law of development of human history ", it obviously cannot be regarded as merely the form in which men became conscious of a transitory conflict, and are going to fight it out. Marx takes this for granted here, and there are other passages in which he speaks of his doctrine as a carrying-over into regions formerly dominated by economically-determined ideologies, of the independent and objective methods of natural science. In practice the essence of Marxian wisdom consists, not in asserting that the " social, political and spiritual life-process in general " is determined by changes in the conditions of production, but in knowing how to distinguish those parts of it which are so determined, from those which are not. It consists in knowing the difference between science and ideology.

Although Marx took this difference for granted, however, he did not clearly define it, and he did not see that it involves an exception to his theory of history. It never seems to have occurred to Marx's mind that history is a generalization which includes the development of the natural sciences. He thought of history as a separate process, which only needed to have its own " inner law " of material motion explained, in order to become itself a natural science beside the others. Hence the fact that the development of natural science stood outside his explanation of history, never troubled him. And that Marxism also stood outside it, although it is clearly implied in this sentence I have quoted, he would unquestionably have denied. It was Marx's opinion that Marxism—which explains all history, and knows both its early beginning and its remote destination, and knows moreover the relation between itself and the contemporary historic process—is nevertheless nothing but a " reflection " of that process. It differs from ideological socialism in being " conscious " of the economic movement of which it is a " necessary reflection ".

This was made perfectly clear by Engels, who did undertake some time after Marx's death, to define the word *ideology* and determine its relation to science. He defined it, in effect, as follows : An ideology is a distorted reflection, which is unconscious of the fact that it is a reflection, of economic conditions. In this definition there is no trace left of the contrast between ideologies as economic reflections and natural science as independent truth, which was implied in Marx's classical statement. With Engels all ideas are economic reflections, and scientific ideas can differ from ideologies only in knowing that they are economic reflections, and being approximately correct ones. The science of astronomy, for instance, instead of being, or somehow or other *besides* being, an accurate reflection of the motion of the stars, must be also—provided it is not mere ideology—a reflection of economic motions on earth. This proposition seems absurd enough when it is applied to astronomy, and that goes to show that Engels, like Marx, never thought of such sciences as having a place *within* history. Their place was beside history ! But Engels did think of the science of Marxism as having a place within history, and he applied that absurd proposition to the Marxism science repeatedly and explicitly. He said that Marxism is nothing but a " reflection in thought of the conflict in fact " between the existing productive forces and the capitalist relations of production.

This statement, if it is taken seriously, does not merely mean that Marx reflected this conflict at those times when he was specifically talking about it. It means that the whole general Marxian science of history, is a reflection of this particular historic fact. It means that when Marx gives us an account of the primitive accumulation of capital, for instance, it is not really, or not " in the last analysis ", certain material facts of past history that his thoughts are reflecting, but it is his own position, or that of the proletariat, in the society in which he lives. And when Engels writes of the Origin of the Family, it is not a reflection of the actual origin of the family, but a reflection in the form of a painstaking and classical book about the origin of the family, of the origin of a revolution in the current mode of production. And in general Marxism is not at every point a reflection of just those facts which it purports to reflect—much less a definition of them " with the exactitude of natural science "—but it is at all points a mystic and scientifically irresponsible reflection of the position of the working class in modern society, a mere " general expression " of the existing class struggle. Moreover when the class struggle is over, Marxism must lose its essential validity and give place to an entirely different science, for it is obvious that a system of ideas which merely reflects the struggles of a class, can play no vital part in reflecting the evolution of a class-free society. That is the real meaning of Engels' statement about Marxism. And it is adopted with admirable boldness by Rosa Luxemburg, who says that " Marxism pretends only to temporary truth ; dialectic through and through, it contains within itself the seeds of its own destruction."

Now everybody who is familiar with scientific method knows that the one thing which can verify Marxism as a science, and establish it among the indubitable and immortal conquests of human knowledge, is the triumph of the proletariat and the establishment of a class-free society. Everybody who is not familiar with scientific method, but is also innocent of metaphysics, knows the same thing. In Russia the first preliminary victory of the proletariat has resulted, not only in a recognition of the verified truths of Marxism, but in a codification and dogmatization and universal systemized adoration of every last letter of Marx's writing, such that, if Marx had imagined it, he would never have dared put pen to paper. It is pure myth-making to say that Marxism will be destroyed by the triumph of the revolution, and it is arrant metaphysical nonsense to pretend that Marxism contains no other truth than the correct reflection of a contemporary change in the conditions of production. This not only contradicts the most important part of Marx's own statement—the part in which he tells us how to study revolutions—but it contradicts the simple and universal facts of human psychology. Just as everyone who thinks practically assumes that the future is in some degree undetermined, so everyone who thinks theoretically assumes that his thoughts are not ultimately determined by any facts other than those contemplated in his theory. He assumes that his thoughts are not ideology but science. They are not the forms in which men have become conscious of a material change, and are going to " fight it out ", but they are the forms in which men have defined a material change and understood it.

The reason why Marxists have blurred the distinction between science and ideology, which is inextricably involved in Marx's classical statement of his theory of history, is that this distinction is inconsistent with Marx's own philosophy of Dialectic Materialism. If thought is merely a reflection of the dialectic motions of matter, there can only be right and wrong reflections, conscious and unconscious reflections. And any given thought at any given time *must* be, somehow or other, a reflection of dialectic motions that are contemporary with it. Science has to be an ideology, according to this system, and the very best it can do is to be a conscious and correct one. This is so obvious that Plekhanov, the unmitigated metaphysician who laid the foundations of Russian Marxism, simply dropped out the distinction between science and ideology altogether, and forgot it. In Russia to-day the word ideology retains not the slightest tincture of the meaning it had for Marx and Engels. For them it was the ultimate form of intellectual abuse. For Russian Marxists it is simply the name for any body of ideas held together by some common bond. Lenin speaks of " the scientific ideology as opposed to the religious ". He defines Marxism as " the ideology of the proletariat instructed by capitalism ". Trotsky says that " in the socialist movement ideology plays its essential and enormous rôle ". And the Russian Bolsheviks in general regard the distinction between communism, for instance, and the principles of democracy, not as a distinction between science and ideological talk, but as a distinction between the " bourgeois " and " proletarian " ideologies.

Plekhanov carried his philosophic rectification of Marx's natural opinion about ideology and science, to the point of asserting that " Das Kapital " itself is not fundamentally more scientific than the bourgeois economics. The fundamental difference between them is that the bourgeois economics reflects an earlier, and the Marxian a later stage in the historic process :

" Human society in its development passes through certain phases to which correspond certain phases of development of social science. That which we call, for example, bourgeois economics is one phase of development of economic science. That which we call socialist economics is another phase of its development immediately following. . . .

" The bourgeois economics, in so far as it corresponds to a definite phase of social evolution, possesses scientific truth. But that truth is relative, exactly because it corresponds only to a certain phase of social development. The bourgeois theoreticians, imagining that society must always remain in its bourgeois phase, attribute absolute significance to that relative truth. In that consists their fundamental mistake, corrected by scientific socialism, the appearance of which testifies that the bourgeois epoch of social development is nearing its end."

This statement is perhaps plausible, so long as you do not remember that Plekhanov's statements themselves *are* scientific socialism. When you remember that, you cannot fail to ask : How does it happen that scientific socialism. which is merely the reflection of another transitory phase of social development, knows all about the whole process of social development, and all about its relation to the bourgeois phase, and in fact all about the ways and phases of the universe in general ? A bourgeois ideologist could reply to Plekhanov : Your science, which declares that everything changes and progresses, is but a reflection of the position of the proletariat in capitalist society ; it is a relative truth ; but my science reflects the eternal relations of the bourgeoisie and the proletariat as they really are ! In simple honesty there would be no answer to this.

And just this difficulty lies at the bottom of the whole structure of Russian Marxism. How can a mere proletarian ideology be a scientific account of the development of the universe and of human history ? Bukharin begins a text-book which is supposed to teach the young Russian how to think, with an argument in a circle which may be summed up as follows : Everything changes ; we, the proletariat, are interested in change ; therefore our philosophy, which asserts that everything changes, is entitled to general belief. That is only a naïve exposure of the fallacy that Plekhanov dressed up so plausibly. And the same fallacy constitutes the deep flaw in Lenin's philosophic writings. Lenin declares that Marx and Engels were " from first to last partisan in philosophy " ;

that philosophy is nothing but a " partisan struggle " between idealism and materialism ; that dialectic materialism is the ideological fortress of the working class, which " would never let petit-bourgeois philistinism step over its threshold " ; he declares that " in a society torn by class contradictions there can be no extra-class or super-class ideology " ; and he illustrates this statement with a book which is the most embattled and violent polemic ever produced in the name of philosophy. And yet in that book he asserts that " the theory of Marx is objective truth ", meaning thereby that " going by way of the Marxian theory we shall draw nearer and nearer to objective truth (never exhausting it) and going by any *other road* we can arrive at nothing but confusion and lies ". To identify objective truth with the fighting ideology of one camp in a pitched battle between classes, and to call this truth philosophy—that is the fundamental fallacy of Russian Marxism.

But Russian Marxism is merely Marxism in its purest Hegelian-metaphysical form. And the reader must not think that this fallacy presents a difficulty which the Hegelian dialectic is unable to squirm out of. On the contrary the Hegelian dialectic was invented for the express purpose of squirming out of such difficulties. It was invented in order to protect the right of a priesthood to identify their emotional interests and those of the class they represent, with objective and absolute truth. And if it is able—by the simple device of standing on its head—to protect an anti-priesthood, and the class they represent, in a similar right, that is but one more tribute to the expert metaphysical genius of its inventor. When you have laid it down that everything which exists is a process of self-contradiction, you are not going to be disturbed by the discovery that your own science is at the same time *objectively true* and *relative to your particular position in history.* That contradiction merely shows that it exists ! And if you have also laid it down that every such self-contradictory process is destined to have its opposing elements reconciled in a " higher " unity—and if you have refrained from laying it down just when, or where, or under what circumstances, any particular part of this business takes place—then you are in a position to assert that the reconciliation between the objective and the relative in scientific truth will take place only after human experience and investigation have been extended to infinity. That infinitely distant reconciliation is Absolute Truth. But since that Absolute Truth is, by definition, a " higher " unity, and since you, who reflect the breakdown of capitalism, are farther along the road to it, than your class opponent who represents capitalism rampant, it is obvious that your ideology is already absolutely true in comparison with his. In fact your ideology is able to denounce and trounce all previous ideologies, because it contains them as surmounted opposites in its own bosom, and is on its way with them to the glory goal of an Absolute that lies at the end of infinity. . . . That is the kind of semi-theological jargon by which Hegel's dialectic enables you to identify a working-class ideology with objective truth, and get along without the practical distinction which Marx drew between science and ideology. More important—that is the kind of semi-theological jargon *for the sake of which* Marx's practical distinction between science and ideology has been thrown away.

CHAPTER VIII

MARXISM AND THE PSYCHOLOGY OF FREUD

YOU have only to abandon mysteries and the relics of mysteries, and introduce into Marxism the simple beginnings of a true science of thought, in order to define ideology accurately, and distinguish it from science, and see that this distinction is the essence of Marx's historical wisdom. It is one of the deepest and wisest intuitions in all the history of genius. Life is impulsive, and thought is a definition of impulse and of the means to its satisfaction. But in human society life's strongest and most universal impulses are suppressed by a standard of ideality and respectable virtue, that is an automatic product of social intercourse and self-consciousness. These strong universal impulses disappear out of men's thoughts, but they do not die. They continue to function unconsciously, and the result is a falsification of the conscious thoughts, wherever they touch a matter in which these suppressed impulses are concerned. Men think they are defending and pursuing such goals as Liberty, Equality, Fraternity, when in reality their concern is, as Marx put it, with Infantry, Cavalry, and Artillery. Their concern is to defend their own privileged position in a class which, in its unconscious but ultimately reliable motivation, knows nothing and cares nothing about liberty, or equality, or fraternity. That is what an ideology is. It is a thinking process which is unaware of the motive which instigated it, and toward the satisfaction of which it is directed. That the great part of written history, and of political and sociological theorizing, up to the time of Marx, was distorted with such ideological thinking, indulged in by people controlled by their own unconscious class interests, is fairly obvious. It is also obvious that this process has not ceased merely because it has been discovered. But it is certainly the ideal and the essence of scientific thinking to escape from it. Practical scientific thinking defines its real motives, because it seeks a clear knowledge of the means to their satisfaction. And " pure " scientific thinking defines its motives, because it wishes to abstract from them, and get a picture of the facts which will be as objective and general as the nature of the human brain permits. Both these kinds of thinking are sharply and unmistakably distinguished, exactly as Marx originally said they are, from economically-determined ideologies.

In short, just as Marx anticipated in his " Theses on Feuerbach " the functional theory of knowledge, so in his doctrine of ideologies he anticipated the psychology of Sigmund Freud. The psycho-analyst, because he is trying to cure individual disorders, emphasizes those distortions of consciousness which arise from suppressed motives of sex. The Marxist, who wishes to cure the disorders of society, emphasizes those which arise from motives of hunger and fighting egoism. It is such motives which unconsciously dominate the majority of men in those broad social and political relations which constitute so large a part of their lives. It is such motives which align them in antagonistic classes, with the result that loyalty to class takes the place of that loyalty to society as a whole, upon which it might be possible to establish the framework of a reasonable world. Marx's word ideology is simply a name for the distortions of social and political thinking which are created by these suppressed motives. It is a general term for all that Freudians mean when they say *rationalization, substitution, transference, displacement, sublimation.* The economic interpretation of history is nothing but a generalized psycho-analysis of the social and political mind. One might infer this from the spasmodic and unreasonable resistance it meets on the part of its patient. The Marxian diagnosis is regarded as an outrage rather than a science. It is met, not with comprehension and critical analysis, but with rationalizations and " defence-reactions " of the most wild and infantile kind.

One of the most notable of these defence-reactions has been contributed by the Freudians themselves. They have invented the device of explaining away all revolutionary intelligence as a manifestation of the " Oedipus complex ". Freud seems to have remained wisely silent upon this theme, but it is quite a fashion among his followers to dismiss any man who wants to cut under the plausibilities of existing law and government, as a neurotic driven on by an unconscious fixation of infantile emotion against his father. It is a case, they say, of *substitution,* or *transference* of the libido. The answer from the Marxian point of view is obvious : Doctors are in the economic nature of things bourgeois, or petit-bourgeois, and these Freudian doctors are driven on, in their attempt to explain away revolution, by unconscious motives of class-loyalty and pecuniary self-defence. It is a case of *ideological thinking.* In this exchange of amenities, the Marxian may have the satisfaction of remembering that Marx got there first. And he has this satisfaction also, that his position does not involve a snap-diagnosis of some of the healthiest and most stable personalities in the world as neurotic, and it does not pretend to an expert opinion on the intimate family history of several millions of people who have never been examined. It attributes to these Freudian doctors no condition more peculiar than the most general underlying motives of all humanity and all organic life.

When I say that the doctrine of ideologies is an anticipation of the Freudian psychology, I mean it literally and exactly. It can be nothing else, once you have put in the place of metaphysical fairy-stories, a science of human thought and behaviour. This can be seen clearly in any of Engels' attempts to state what an ideology is. " An ideology," he says in one place, " is a process which is carried out, to be sure, with the consciousness of the so-called thinker, but with a false consciousness. The real motive-powers which move him remain unknown to him, otherwise it would not be an ideological process." You need only recognize that the motive-powers which move people to think are organic impulses, or " desires ", and you have here all the essentials of a Freudian definition. And there are passages, indeed, where both Marx and Engels do seem to recognize this fact. In his book about the " Eighteenth Brumaire of Louis Bonaparte ", where Marx applies his theory to a piece of concrete historic action, he continally talks of the " interests " of the classes and parties concerned. He interprets their political ideas, not as an unconscious reflection of their economic position, but as an unconscious scheme for getting their economic wishes satisfied.

" As in private life we distinguish between what a man thinks and says about himself, and what he really is and does, still more in historical struggles we must distinguish the phrases and imaginations of parties from their real organism and their real interests. . . . Thus the Tories in England long imagined that they were raving about the Kingdom, the

Church, and the Beauty of the Old-English dispensation, until the day of danger snatched from them the confession that they were only raving about Ground Rent."

That this is Freudian psychology at its most brilliant, needs no demonstration. Engels in his speech at the grave of Marx described the whole Marxian theory of history as a discovery of " the simple fact, heretofore concealed under ideological overgrowths, that men have first of all to eat and drink and live and clothe themselves, and only after that can they occupy themselves with politics and science and art and religion. . . ." Here again it is simply the underlying animal motivation that explains history ; Marx's theory appears as a study of human behaviour, and not a searching among human " accidents " for the mysterious march of an animated generality called Forces of Production. And ideologies in consequence play exactly the part that is played by rationalizations in a Freudian psychology. They serve as concealments in consciousness, for those crude unconscious motives which on the broad average and in the long run determine the conduct of men.

For Marx and Engels, however, these occasional statements of human motivation were not the true, the esoteric, science of history. The true science demands that human motives should be seen as merely a specific part of that more general motor process, the Evolution of the Forces of Production, which takes the place of Hegel's " Spirit ". Engels describes in the following passage the relation of human motives to the historic process :

" History proceeds in such a way that the end-result always issues from the conflict of many individual wills. . . . We have thus innumerable conflicting forces, an endless group of parallelograms of forces, giving a resultant—the historic event—which may itself again be regarded as the product of a force acting as a whole without consciousness and without will.   For that which each individual desires, meets an opposition from every other, and the result is something which nobody desired."

That is the inscrutable way in which history operates, according to metaphysical Marxism.   And it is obvious that a psychological analysis would be an awkward intrusion here.   For that " result " which " nobody desired ", is exactly the heart's desire of the Marxian metaphysician.   And it is the essence of his " materialist " metaphysics to assert that the objective world is going after it and getting it for him without thought and without will—albeit by a process that is " logical ", and with a " determinism " that is hard to distinguish from the most wilful determination.

Thus when Marx and Engels employ the language of human motivation in their explanation of history, it must· be regarded as a temporary condescension from the abstract perfection of the pure theory.   The " inner laws " of history are not to be discovered by talking in this way.   And when Engels says that the ideologist is unconscious of the forces that set his thoughts going, it must not be imagined that he means to psycho-analyse that ideologist, or say that he is not conscious of his own motives.   All he means to say is that the ideologist is not conscious of a motion in the " economic conditions ", which are a result of the evolution of the " productive-forces ", and of which his thoughts are a mere passive reflection.

" The reflection of economic relations in the form of legal principles is accomplished in such a way that this process does not reach the consciousness of the agent.   The law-maker imagines that he is acting from a priori principles, when in reality it is all a matter of economic reflection . . . and that distortion, when it is not conscious, we call the ideological outlook."

That is the way Engels defines ideology in a more painstaking moment. And again :

" That the material conditions of life of the men in whose heads this thinking process takes place, ultimately determine the course of the process, necessarily remains unknown to these men, otherwise there would be an end of the whole ideology."

It seems a very slight and obvious correction to say *material interests* here, instead of " material conditions of life ", but it is all the difference between science and mystical metaphysics. And it was nothing but mystical metaphysics which prevented Engels from saying it. Nothing but mystical metaphysics will prevent any Marxian from abandoning this " Philosophy of History ", and going forward to that more analytical scientific attitude which it anticipated. It will be objected, of course, that " psychology is in its infancy ", that nobody can put his trust in these vague beginnings of a science of the mind. It is true that psychology is in its infancy ; it is true that we have only the first loose principles of a science of the mind. But the philosophy of Dialectic Materialism rests upon the assumption that a hundred years ago Hegel knew all about mind, and substantially finished the science of it. The philosophy of Dialectic Materialism lives or dies with that assumption. Therefore if the real science of the mind is in its infancy, the philosophy of Dialectic Materialism may best be described as dead. Better an infant science that is alive, than a dead metaphysics.

CHAPTER IX

IDEOLOGY AND THE ART OF REVOLUTION

THE concept of ideology not only contains the essence of Marx's contribution to the general science of history, but it reveals most exactly his innovation in the particular science and art of revolution. Marx's word " ideology " was invented by Napoleon Bonaparte for the express purpose of deriding revolutionary idealism. " It was a nickname," to quote an early biographer, " which the French ruler used to distinguish every species of theory, which resting in no respect upon the basis of self-interest, could, he thought, prevail with none save hot-brained boys and crazed enthusiasts." That is to say, it was an epitome of the counter-revolutionary propaganda. It was a summing up in one word of what all hard-headed practical men of the world have said about social idealists from the beginning of time. They have said that they are mere emotional enthusiasts who " don't know any-thing about human nature ". And up to the time of Marx these statements had been in a broad sense correct. Marx took the hard-headed practical realistic sagacity of these " men of the world ", and introduced it into the ranks of the revolution. Marxism is hard-headed idealism. It is idealism taking account of the facts. It is Napoleonic ruthlessness on the other side of the barricade. And that is why Marx instinctively adopted Napoleon's term of derision for all thinking which is detached from the facts, and which ignores those egoistical-economic motives that constitute the main driving force in history. He wanted to get the same foolish and utopian nonsense out of his way that Napoleon did, but for an opposite purpose.

Marx achieved this hard-headed condition, as we have seen, by projecting his own emotional idealism into the external world. He had been taught in a German university to regard the universe as an idealistic development, an " endless passing from the lower to the higher ". He scrutinized and rejected much of what he learned in that university, but he never scrutinized this word " higher ", nor endangered his entire intellectual equilibrium by asking himself what it really meant. It meant, so far as concerns human history at least, *nearer to his own emotional ideals*. Marx was able to treat these ideals with Napoleonic scorn, at the same time that he consecrated his life to them, because he regarded their appearance in his mind as merely a " symptom " of what an accommodating universe was about to do in regard to them.

" The appeal to morality and justice does not bring us forward a finger's breadth scientifically ; economic science can see no proof in moral indignation, be it never so justified, but only a symptom. The task of this science is rather to explain the newly arising social evils as necessary consequences of the existing mode of production, but also at the same time as signs of its approaching dissolution, and to discover within the economic movement-form which is dissolving, the elements of the future new organization of production and exchange, which will abolish those evils."

It is easy to scorn your own ideals, treating them as mere signs of a crisis in the evolution of material forces, when you have already confided the attainment of your ideals to those material forces. That was the hard-headedness of Marx and Engels. It was only in a world which was evolving " by its own inevitable dialectic " toward something " higher ", toward something " more magnificent ", that they knew how to be Napoleonic and dismiss ideologies altogether.   To be hard-headed in this real world, which cares nothing at all about what you consider higher, and yet at the same time be idealistic and fight to make something higher out of it, is a little more difficult.   But it is the task ultimately laid on us by that course of scientific reasoning which Marx began. It is impossible, once you understand the psychology of the process, to continue this grandiose pretence at a dispassionate reflection of mere economic necessities, which is so often repeated in the writings of Marx and Engels, and so often betrayed.   It is impossible, once you have defined ideology as thinking which is unconscious of its motive, to let Marxism continue to hide its motive in an animistic philosophy of the universe. Marxism as a system of dialectic metaphysics *is* ideological, just as all metaphysics is, but it is certainly the tendency and the true end of Marxism to become a science.

CHAPTER X

MARXIAN ECONOMICS

IT is difficult to draw a line between the ideological and the scientific element in economic theory. The subject-matter here is the very essence of the egoistic struggle of men, a preoccupation of their unconscious natures. And the science is of necessity abstract and indefinite. It is a matter of formulating large groups of facts, rather than accurately defining particulars, and in this act of formulation the hidden purpose of the scientist has a very free hand. However, if an economist who acknowledged a revolutionary purpose, and one who acknowledged a conservative purpose, sat down to formulate the laws upon which they could agree, we should still have something of an objective science of economics. And it is only by conceiving this science as a thing apart from the expressions of class-interest which have been bound up in it, that we can adequately describe the economic contributions of Karl Marx. He contributed certain fundamental and enduring ideas or attitudes to the science of economics, and he replaced the business man's ideology that is usually bound up in that science with a proletarian ideology.

Perhaps the most indubitable contribution of Marx to economic theory, was the idea implied in our current use of the word " capitalism ". Marx was the first to realize the full extent of the evolution that has taken place in human industry. He realized that many of the most fundamental of those " Laws of Political Economy ", which so startled the intellectual world in the eighteenth century, were but laws of that capitalistic system of economy which had begun its existence about two hundred years before. He conceived of economics as a genuinely historical science, and traced the development of modern capitalistic business out of the previous systems of production and exchange. Viewing it in this evolutionary way, Marx was able to describe clearly certain features of " capitalism " that were not adequately perceived by previous economists. That the productive process had become co-operative, or " social ", and was becoming more and more so, as a result of the factory system and the invention of modern machinery, was a thing which Marx first clearly realized. And he realized the full extent to which this social process would come to be concentrated in vast organizations under the control of a few men. He " predicted the trusts ", as Marxians are accustomed to say. If there is in academic circles a reluctance to acknowledge these contributions, or the source of them, that reluctance may properly be described as ideological. The contributions were scientific. They were contributions to the definition of objective facts, and they belong neither to the capitalists nor to the proletariat. They are among the common assumptions of all real political intelligence.

But Marx not only perceived more clearly than others how profoundly the economic process has changed in the last three or four hundred years. He also perceived the essential feature in which it has not changed—the continued exploitation of the labouring masses by a possessing class. He perceived that the wage-worker in our capitalist system of industry works a part of the time for himself and a part of the time for his master, just as truly as the villein did under the feudal system. Our system of " free competition " and cash payment for labour, conceals this fact, and all our laws and political principles, and our most honoured thoughts about the matter, are concerned to disguise it. But the fact remains. And it was a characteristic achievement of Marx's genius to lay it bare. It was an application of that distinction between science and ideology which I have described as the essence of his contribution to the study of history. Marx himself felt that this was the most original and most important thing in his system of economics. In a letter written to Engels soon after the publication of the first volume of " Capital ", he stated what were the new things of fundamental importance in it. Here is what he said :

" First, that in contrast to all former economists, who from the beginning treat the separate fragments of surplus value with their fixed forms of rent, profit, interest as something given, I treat first of all the general form of surplus value, wherein all the as yet undistinguished forms find themselves, so to speak, in solution. Second, that economists without exception ignore the simple fact that if commodities have a two-fold value, then also the labour embodied in commodities must possess a two-fold character ; the mere analysis into labour *sans phrase* as with Smith, Ricardo, etc., landing us on the whole in the inexplicable. This is in fact the whole secret of the critical view. Third, that for the first time the labour-wage is expounded as the irrational phenomenal form of a relation concealed behind it."

Translated into the language of concrete intelligence, these three points all mean that the worker in our capitalist society works part of the time for himself and part of the time for the owners of the instruments with which he works, and that all of the income of the possessing classes, whether directly received in the form of rent, profit or interest, comes ultimately, just as the wealth of the feudal nobility did, from the work which the worker does, not for himself, but for his master, and not for a product but for a profit. This statement is not true in the absolute form in which Marx's philosophy compelled him to make it. But the facts upon which it is based are sufficiently general, and have been sufficiently ignored by other economists, to warrant the assertion that Marx introduced into the objective science of economics—supposing that one could find such a thing—an adequate recognition of the state of affairs designated by the term " wage slavery ".

That Marx should have to write a letter to his best friend, telling what the essential proposition is, which he had just finished expounding in a volume of eight hundred pages, and that this letter in turn should require interpretation in order to make it in the least degree intelligible to a man of ordinary education, may suggest to the reader that the intellectual method adopted in the Marxian economics is not of the best. And I advise him to give free scope to the suggestion. Marx's " Capital " combines the principal vices of the classical German philosophy with the principal vices of the classical British Economy. In that sense it is indeed a classic, and has inevitably found its way, along with so many other classics, to the top shelves of a great many libraries. It contains a wealth of interesting ideas, and much invaluable empirical material—a study of the development of modern industry in England that ought to be dissected out and published as one of the most significant chapters of human history. But as a " System of Economics " it must inevitably retire, along with the rest of that classical economy and that classical philosophy to whose tradition it belongs, into the position of an intellectual " object of art ", an ingenious and fertile historic curiosity. For it is not in its fundamental form and theoretic substance a scientific book.

It is not, except incidentally, an exposition and empirical demonstration of that concrete fact about the exploitation of labour under capitalism which Marx saw so clearly. It is a flying upward from that concrete fact into the world of unreal abstractions contemplated by the classical economy, and an attempt to make it *reappear* there with an emotional glamour and a metaphysical significance greater than any simple statement of concrete facts could have.

The classical economy had settled, in Marx's day, upon a conception of the " value " of commodities —the rate at which they exchange on the market—as ultimately determined by the labour necessary to their production. It had also arrived at a problem of explaining according to this conception the value of labour itself, which seems to sell on the market just like any of these commodities whose value it determines. The value of labour ought also to be determined by the amount of labour necessary to produce it. But that is a useless, if not indeed a meaningless proposition, which merely reduces the given conception of value to absurdity. Marx invented a way out of this difficulty. He thought up the idea of saying that the thing which is for sale on the market is not labour, but " labour-power ". The capitalist may be said to buy this commodity at a rate determined, as much as that of any other commodities, by the amount of labour necessary to produce it. But this commodity has the peculiar property of creating value, and if put into contact with machinery and raw materials, it will create a value very much greater than its own. And that " surplus value " created by the labourer for the capitalist who has bought his labour power as a commodity, will explain, with all the neatness of the classical economy, how people get rich in our society by merely producing and exchanging " commodities " whose value is by definition equivalent. In this way Marx succeeded in fixing up the abstract formulation of the process of capitalistic production attempted by Smith and Ricardo upon the basis of a labour explanation of value, in such a way as to make an emphasis upon the exploitation of labour just as abstract, and just as " classical ", as any of their more conservative constructions.

There is no denying the ingenuity and interestingness of the idea. But it is absurd to attribute to this ingenious manipulation of abstractions a weight and significance comparable to that possessed by the simple concrete fact which made it possible—the fact that the earth and the instruments of production belong to a few people, and they get rich, on the whole, by compelling other people to work for them at approximately a living wage. The classical economy has fallen out of scientific repute, not because it was wholly at variance with the facts, but because it was not sufficiently interested in them. The principal object of its study was the relations between a set of abstract ideas. And Marx's economic system shares the fate of the classical economy, because it shares the same fault. Indeed, it carries that fault to an unheard of extreme. Marx makes it clear in his very first chapter that a " commodity " is an abstraction, that " value " in the sense in which he uses the term is an abstraction, and that the " labour " which constitutes this value is something that never existed on land or sea. It is " abstract human labour " of the " average degree of skill and intensity prevalent at the time ". And nevertheless his mind is satisfied to describe commodities as the " material depositories of exchange value ", to describe this value as " abstract human labour . . . in a congealed state ", as in fact " crystals of this social substance ", a " homogeneous jelly " composed of something which by definition does not exist. He treats abstract and concrete labour as two " different kinds " of labour, and declares that in a commodity which is regarded as the equivalent of another in an act of exchange, " concrete labour becomes the form under which its opposite, abstract labour, manifests itself ". It would be difficult to find in the whole history of science a more mystical and unreal construction. Marx himself confessed that he " coquetted " with a Hegelian phraseology in this chapter. The fact is that only a man trained from childhood not only in this phraseology, but in the sincere conviction that the real world is composed of abstract and general ideas alienated from themselves in material objects, and who had never essentially recovered from that training, could possibly have conceived or written such a chapter, or regarded the propositions which he deduced from it, or professed in whole or in part to deduce from it, as having the character of empirical science.

That Marx's disquisitions about value and surplus value—in spite of the indubitable concrete fact out of which they are fabricated—are not scientific generalizations, is practically conceded by Marx himself in the third volume of his " Capital ". At least that is my opinion— which I ought to warn the reader is amateur and inexpert in matters of economic theory—about this famous subject of dispute. In this third volume Marx comes down to the question of the rates at which concrete and visible objects actually sell upon the market, and of the profits actually made by concrete and visible capitalists who employ labour. And he is compelled to concede that his laws of value and surplus value are not a definition or explanation of these actual things. They are not generalizations of fact capable of experimental verification. They are a " penetration ", as he says, of the " outward disguise " constituted by these concrete facts, " into the internal essence and inner form of the capitalist process of production ". To an empirically and really scientific mind these words " internal " and " inner "—which come to the rescue not only here, but at every moment of critical danger in the Marxian metaphysics—mean nothing in the world but *abstract*. To such a mind, therefore, this statement is an abandonment by Marx of his own pretence to have formulated the laws of the concrete process of capitalist production. It is a confession that he is not talking about these concrete facts. The boast of Engels that " the classical economy had got lost in a blind alley—the man to find the way out was Karl Marx ", is perhaps true. But Marx found his way out, as was inevitable to anyone adopting the same methods, into another blind alley. The only way to escape from these blind alleys, is to abandon the deductive and rationalistic methods common to Marx and the classical economists, cease to delude ourselves that when in the process of abstraction we draw farther away from the variety of the concrete facts, we are " penetrating " into the " inward essence " of those facts, and come back to an attitude of experimental humility before the facts themselves.

CHAPTER XI

IDEOLOGY IN " DAS KAPITAL "

THE reason why Marxists, who are so devoted in other matters to the maxim that " The truth is always concrete ", are just the last ones to give up overvaluing the abstractions of pure economics, is that there is bound up for them in that science a proletarian ideology. They do not approach " Das Kapital " as social engineers, desirous to find out the real structure and movement of the world they are working with. If they did, they would be as intolerant of its indirectness, its lumbersome, long-winded intellectualism and perfectly unnecessary obscurity, as anybody else. They come to it as adherents of a faith, desirous to be convinced that the " inner hidden laws " of this world are working with them. Obviously then, the more " inner " these laws are, the more " hidden " they are, the better, the more convincing, the more easily defended against those who are deceived by the " visible external movement " of things.

The classical political economy had also contained an ideological element. In order to formulate its laws of production and exchange, it had made the assumption that every man acts in all business relations upon a motive of reasoned self-interest. And the neatness and convincingness of the structure which it built upon this assumption were so astonishing, that it did not seem absurd to tack on to it the assertion that this " reasonable self-interest " of every individual is a very fine thing, which if only left to itself would automatically produce the welfare of society as a whole. This assertion was obviously not a part of the science of economics ; it was the ideology of a thriving business class. As there is not any welfare of society as a whole, nor even any enduring welfare of the business class, this ideology did not last very long in its pure form. Various measures of social and political reform began to seem more satisfactory in its place. But the general assumption that those " laws " of capitalistic business describe what must be and ought to be, as well as what is, continues to characterize the academic science of economics even to-day. It is on the one hand an attempt at a scientific generalization, and on the other an ideological justification of the fundamental structure of capitalist society.

Marx put his proletarian ideology exactly in the place of that original ideology of the business class. In place of the assertion that the instinctive economic activities of men automatically produce social welfare, he put the assertion that these same activities automatically produce a social revolution. His dialectic philosophy of history had perfectly prepared him for this. His conception that when men enter into social relations, an ordered development arises which is wholly independent of their consciousness and their wills, was far more dependable for this purpose than the concept of the " Economic Man ". It left Marx free from that criticism from the standpoint of realism in psychology, which has spoiled the beauty, and practically broken the authority, of the classical Economics. Marx himself abandoned the " Economic Man ", as his defenders are careful to explain. But Marx abandoned the Economic Man, not because he wished to make a closer analysis of the concrete facts, but because he wished to stay farther away from them. He abandoned the Economic Man, because he had an Economic God—the self-active Dialectic Development of the Forces of Production—who was far more reliable for ideological purposes than anything so specific and dubious as a formula for human nature. The Marxian ideology consists of fitting the abstractions of the Classical Political Economy, as amended but not transcended by Marx, into Hegel's philosophy of the universe as a dialectic evolution of abstractions—this also amended, but not transcended by Marx—and thus arriving at a mystical conviction of the " iron necessity " of the revolution that he desired.

Perhaps the easiest way to see how this was accomplished, is to study the thing in its origin. In the " Holy Family ", a book completed by Marx and Engels four years before they formulated their opinions in the Communist Manifesto, Marx has the following passage :

" Proletariat and wealth are opposites. As such they form a whole. They are both phases of the world of private property. It is a question of the definite position which they both occupy in the antithesis. It is not enough to declare them two sides of a whole.

" Private property as private property, as wealth, is compelled to preserve itself, and therewith its opposite, the proletariat. It is the positive side of the antithesis, private property satisfied with itself.

" The proletariat, on the contrary, as proletariat is compelled to annihilate itself, and therewith its conditioning opposite which makes it a proletariat, private property. It is the negative side of the antithesis, its dissatisfaction with itself, private property dissolved and dissolving itself . . .

" Thus within the antithesis the private property-owner is the conservative, the proletarian the destructive part. From the former comes the motion to preserve the antithesis, from the latter the motion to destroy it.

" Private property, to be sure, impels itself in its national economic movement to its own dissolution, but only through a development independent of itself, unconscious, and taking place against its will, a development involved in the nature of the case—only through the fact that it creates the proletariat as proletariat, misery conscious of its spiritual and physical misery, inhumanity conscious of its inhumanity and therefore annihilating itself. The proletariat fulfills the sentence pronounced upon itself by wage-labour in creating another's wealth and its own misery. When the proletariat triumphs, it then by no means becomes the absolute side of society, since it triumphs only in that it annihilates itself and its opposite. The proletariat itself disappears no less than its conditioning opposite, private property."

It is quite obvious in this most perfect of " dialectic constructions " that the only dynamic force—the only thing which prevents it all from standing still right where it is—is the Hegelian Logic. All existing things or subjects of discourse, are self-contradictions, and all self-contradictions are bound by *a logical necessity* to resolve themselves in a higher unity. Therefore when you have shown the given subject of discourse, capitalist society, to be a self-contradiction, you are under no necessity to prove that it will be resolved in a higher unity. You may show how it will be resolved, but that is merely a matter of logical deduction, and not a problem in dynamics.

Of course Marx outgrew this naïve and ludicrously metaphysical way of expressing himself. He learned, as all good classical philosophers do, to mix the facts and the animistic presuppositions so intricately that it takes a lifetime to divide them. But just the same he did not move one step from his original position, so far as concerns empirically proving the dynamics of his inevitable revolution. His theorizing about the abstract idea of surplus value helped him in the conviction that class-conflict, which he saw to be from the standpoint of his practical effort the *most important* feature of capitalist society, was also from the standpoint of pure knowledge the *inward essence* of it. But it was the Hegelian philosophy, with its assertion that the inward essence of " everything " is conflict, and that all conflicts are bound to be resolved in " higher unities ", which assured him that his practical effort would succeed. In " Das Kapital ", as in the " Holy Family ", the force which guarantees the evolution of capitalism to the point of rupture and the creation of the communist state, is that same logical necessity of ascending from the lower to the higher, which Hegel laid on the whole universe in the name of God.

" Self-earned private property," we read, " based on a fusion, so to speak, of the separate independent working individual with the conditions essential to his work, was supplanted by capitalist private property which rests upon the exploitation of the formally free labour of others.

" As soon as this process of transformation has adequately disintegrated the old society from top to bottom, as soon as the workers are changed into proletarians, and the conditions essential to their labour into capital, as soon as the capitalist mode of production stands upon its own feet, then the further socialization of labour, and the further transformation of the earth and other means of production into socially exploited and therefore communal means of production, hence the further expropriation of the private property-owner, takes a new form. That which is now to be expropriated is no longer the self-managing worker, but the capitalist exploiting many workers.

" This expropriation is accomplished by the play of the immanent laws of capitalist production itself, by the central-ization of capital. One capitalist kills many. Hand in hand with this centralization, or the expropriation of many capi-talists by a few, there develops the co-operative form of the labour-process upon an ever-growing scale, the conscious technical application of science, the systematic exploitation of the soil, the transformation of the means of labour into a means only to be employed in common, the economizing of the means of production through their use as a means of combined social labour, the entanglement of all people in the net of the world-market, and therewith the international character of the capitalist regime. With the continually diminishing number of the magnates of capital, who usurp and monopolize all the advantages of this process of transformation, the mass of misery, oppression, slavery, degradation, exploitation increases, but there increases also the revolt of the working class, perpetually swelling, and schooled, united, organized, by the very mechanism of the capitalist process of production. The monopoly of capital becomes a fetter upon the mode of production which came to its bloom with it and under it. The centralization of the means of production and the socialization of labour reach the point where they become incompatible with their capitalist shell. The shell bursts. The hour of capitalist private property strikes. The expropriators are expropriated.

"The capitalist mode of appropriation, growing out of the capitalist mode of production, and hence capitalist private property, is the first negation of individual private property founded upon the individual's labour. But capitalist production begets with the necessity of a natural process its own negation. It is the negation of the negation. This does not reinstate private property, but just individual ownership on the basis of the achievements of the capitalist era : co-operation and the common possession of the earth and the means of production which are themselves produced by labour."

Disregarding the empirical analysis of capitalism in this passage—the formulation of historic and contemporary facts—ask only where is located, or whence derived, the dynamic force which gives certainty of the motion into the future of this self-contradictory institution. That dynamic force is simply not to be found. Unless you have already the habit of assuming that all that group of facts denoted by the general term "mode of production" are destined by a mystical necessity to evolve upward, you find no reason here why the shell of capitalism should inevitably burst. Unless you know through some avenue that is above the empirical determination of facts, that *all contradictions* are bound to resolve themselves in a higher unity, there is no proof in these facts that "capitalist production creates with the necessity of a natural process the negation of itself ". There is no proof here, and contrary to a common belief, there is no proof anywhere in Marx's " Capital ". In this book as elsewhere, it is by conceiving the class struggle as a contradiction between two generalizations—the capitalist forces of production and the capitalist production-relations—and inferring the victory of the proletariat as a logical conclusion according to the Hegelian system, that Marx arrives at that " iron necessity " of socialism, which is supposed to rest upon the overwhelming assemblage and analysis of facts in " Das Kapital ". It rests upon the relics of religious metaphysics ; it has no other foundation.

The Hegelian philosophy, which professed to portray an eternally fluid and evolving universe, nevertheless managed to bring that universe to a stationary goal in the knowledge of this very Hegel's philosophy, and the tempered blessings of the limited monarchy so generously and so long promised by his gracious sovereign, Frederick William the Third. And Marx's equally fluid although material universe, boasting an equally perfect and eternal evolution, comes to a dead stop when the dictatorship of the proletariat over the bourgeoisie has been resolved by the formation of " an association which excludes classes and their antagonisms ". Is it a mere coincidence that Marx's economic and inward knowledge of the laws of history cannot extend a little forward towards another contradiction, or that it does not fall a little short, or lose a trifle of its iron certainty, before that perfect point is reached ? Is it not quite obvious that it is not Marx's knowledge, but his purpose, that is being expressed ?

Newton's Law of Gravitation, which can be stated in one simple sentence, and upon the verification of which the whole scientific mind of man may be said to have been working, disinterestedly and without ulterior purpose, for two hundred and fifty years, is now called into question in the light of newly discovered facts. And yet the Hegelian Marxist asks us, in the name of " natural science ", to believe that this ponderous philosophico-economical construction, comprised in three enormous volumes, in no one of which is anything so clear as the political passion of its authors, is a sure and accurate statement of the exact law of development of all human history, whose " iron necessity " can be depended on up to and including that " leap from the kingdom of necessity into the kingdom of freedom ", which is a perfect utopian name for the communist society. It is a stultification of the mind to believe it. Marx's " Capital " has been called " The working-man's Bible ", and no more true and fundamental criticism of it can be made than that. It is a book in which the working class can find not only the " most adequate expression of its conditions and its aspirations "—to quote the phrase of Engels—but also the assurance that these have their due place in a universal scheme of evolution toward something better, and that in the due course of history, with a necessity that is absolute if not divine, they are to be satisfied and fulfilled. They are to be satisfied on this earth, and not in heaven. The God who is to satisfy them is not a Loving Father, but a Passionless Process. The mystery which surrounds him is not emotional, but intellectual. And the mode of communion with him is not prayer, but terribly confusing hard work with the brain. These are the principal distinctions between Marx's " Capital " and other kinds of Bibles, and they are not fundamental. They are not comparable to the distinction between a Bible and a text-book in Mechanical Engineering. That book tells you how to do something, it does not tell you what is going to be done.

If Marx had understood the art of practical thinking, " Das Kapital " might have been as great a book as the Hegelian Marxians think it is. And one aspect of its greatness would have been its brevity. It takes a long time to get your passionate purposes thoroughly wound up and lost in a " mental reflection " of the material world. But it does not take so long to set forth the features of that world which are relevant to the attainment of your purposes. " Das Kapital " contains the material necessary to prove that our system of production for profit through the exploitation of labour is inexpedient and uncivilized, and undesirable to anyone who takes the view-point of a true and free human society. And it also contains the material necessary to prove that this system is unstable, and will with practical certainty give rise to imperialistic wars and other crises of a potentially revolutionary character. Indirectly it justifies the revolutionary purpose of Marx, and warrants his belief in the practical possibilities of the class struggle. Taken just as it is, however, the merit of " Das Kapital " lies chiefly in a certain honorific intellectual decoration that it has bestowed upon the workers' movement. It has shown that a professor of revolution can be just as erudite and irrelevant as any other professor. To offset this, it has put upon the revolutionary propagandist the task of defending a thesis absolutely unessential to his task, and wholly beyond the power of the human mind to prove.

CHAPTER XII

THE DIALECTIC METHOD

ACCOMPLISHED Marxists, besides knowing the universe to be a dialectic process, are supposed to possess a dialectic method of thinking, which is appropriate to such a universe, and which constitutes the essence of revolutionary wisdom. Let us examine this " method of thinking " in its origin and development.

The dialectic philosophy as we have seen was a bold manœuvre in the defence of animism against science. Science has always occupied itself with changes, and animism has survived for the most part as an assertion of the Changeless which lies behind and beyond them. As science more and more invades and occupies the mind, however, this Changeless becomes more and more dubious. It becomes less and less interesting. It is a dying God. Hegel revived it by saying that it *is* Change —the one immortal, absolute, *unchanging* Principle— and that it does not dwell behind, or beyond, but *in* the subject-matter of science. If he had left the matter there, however, his manœuvre would not have been successful, for he would merely have transferred into the laboratories of science all the consecrated enthusiasm which he was trying to save for the Church. He had to have some mode of communion with this God, which is the subject-matter of science, besides science itself, which is a matter-of-fact investigation of His various parts and modes of procedure, and a rather irreverent attempt to control

them. He had to have a religious ceremony. And that
was the original function of what is called " dialectic
thinking ".

It is obvious that real thinking, whose function is to
adjust us to the particular parts of a changing world and
enable us to " manage " them, is not very well adapted
to the task of reproducing in our minds the exact nature
of this world as a whole. The only way to manage a world
of change is to discover reliable uniformities, and establish fixed points, within it. And that is what real thinking
does. It forms concepts with fixed meanings and fixed
logical relations to each other, and it applies these fixed
concepts to a world which is not fixed. They do some
violence to the world—they falsify it to some extent—
but they enable us to get along with it. And their fixity
in contrast with its flux, is exactly what gives these concepts their value. Intellectual people, however, who live
among ideas as though they were things, and may be
likened in that respect to insane people, usually forget
this fact. They get to imagining that logical concepts
can be strung together in such a form that they will
actually somehow *reproduce* reality, or to use the phrase
of Engels, " represent the exact nature of the universe ".
And having devised this neat fancy, they are seriously
disturbed when something reminds them that it is not
so. They are disturbed when you point out, for instance,
that the very fact of motion is a little illogical. A body
logically " must be ", you say, at any given moment
either in one place or another, and therefore it logically
cannot be at any given moment on its way from one to
the other. An unintellectual, and as you may say, *natural*
person, is not bothered by this observation, because he
knows that motion is a fact, and the business of thinking
is to deal with facts, and not lay down laws for them.
When reality slips out of the grip of logic, that is to the

natural mind a joke, and not a difficulty. But to the learned intellectual who seeks to contain the universe in his thoughts, or at least put it away on the shelves of his library, the accident is serious. And so he is prepared for the assertion of some deep-voiced and obscure Philosopher of History, that his very method of thinking is inadequate and elementary, and that in order to receive into his mind the exact reality of a world of change, he must have a new kind of Liquefied Logic, called Hegelian. . . . Or he is prepared for some more limpid but equally sonorous Philosopher of Biology, who tells him that logic must be transcended entirely, and a new kind of Vital Intuition, called Bergsonian, put in its place. It makes no difference. He is prepared to be led out of the laboratory and into the temple.

Hegel availed himself of the fact that thought is *not* a mere reproduction of the flux of reality, in order to establish in good scientific repute, and yet over and above science, his religious ceremony of " dialectic thinking ", which pretends that it is a reproduction of the flux of reality. He was thus able to save the essence of animism —its peculiar mode of communion with an external world —and yet concede that the subject-matter of science really is the substance of this world. He was able to combine the comforts of rationalistic religion with a hard empirical realism. He attacked the mystics, he attacked all forms of the idea of transcendent being, as harshly as any merchant-chemist would. But in proportion as he attacked the idea of transcendent being, he emphasized the idea of transcendent thinking—the ineffable logic, the mystery of the philosopher's disciplined meditation, which gives us the pure essence of that evolving God of whom science itself is but an inherent part. And he declared with noble sincerity for all who wish to know, that this speculative logic—this peculiar disciplined mystery of thinking, called philosophy—" is itself a Divine Service, is a religion ".

It seems strange that Marx and Engels, who were so fond of the saying of Feuerbach that " the metaphysician is but a priest in disguise ", should have been completely hookwinked by a metaphysician who frankly abandoned the disguise. But it is a fact which can be established by examining any one of the official expositions of the Marxian " dialectic method ". It is not a method of thinking ; you could not learn one definite thing about the practical art of thinking by reading these expositions. It is the relic of a religious-intellectual ceremony which has been preserved, over and above the practical business of thinking, and for a different purpose. Engels, in his chapter on the dialectic, calls the Negation of the Negation " an extremely far-reaching and important law of development of Nature. . . ." But he speaks with high scorn of the idea that Marx used this law in order to prove anything.

" It shows a complete lack of insight into the nature of the dialectic when Herr Dühring takes it for an instrument of mere proof. . . . The dialectic, besides transcending the narrow horizon of formal logic, contains the germ of a more comprehensive view of the world."

And again :

" With the mere knowledge that the stalk of barley and infinitesimal calculation fall under the law of the Negation of the Negation, I can neither successfully raise barley, nor differentiate and integrate. . . ."

Is it not rather naïve, in expounding an important and far-reaching law of nature, to confess, first, that your law of nature does not enable you to prove anything, and second, that it does not enable you to do or produce anything—and this, too, in a philosophy which declares that " in practice man must prove the truth—the reality, power, this-worldliness, of his thoughts " ? A law of nature is a statement that under such and such circumstances such a thing will happen, or that if I do a certain thing, I shall get a certain result. Could Engels make it clearer that the Negation of the Negation is not a law of nature ? It is a loose and not even poetically interesting analogy between certain curiosities of abstract thinking, and a way of viewing certain natural processes—a thing completely inconsequential to any person not in need upon emotional grounds of a super-scientific mode of " knowing " the perfect Reality.

In another passage Engels plainly declares that ordinary practical thinking is all right for " everyday purposes ", but it is inadequate to the task of giving an " exact representation of the universe. . . ." It is inadequate because it draws a sharp distinction between such things, for instance, as plant and animal, alive and dead, cause and effect. Every jurist knows that you cannot determine an exact moment at which a man ceases to be alive and becomes dead. Every biologist knows that the distinction between plant and animal breaks down among the elementary forms of life. And everybody in the world knows that what is regarded in one connection as an effect, has to be regarded in another connection as a cause. Nature slips out of our fixed concepts ; nothing is more certain than this fact. But the thought which recognizes this fact, is just the same kind of thought as any other. The inferences to be drawn from it, must be drawn in the same way as other inferences. And the inference of Engels that we must try to introduce into those fixed concepts themselves the fluidity and logical unreliability of nature, has no warrant whatever in the fact. Our idea of alive, he says, in effect, should also be an idea of dead, our idea of plant should include that of animal, and our antithesis between cause and effect, which " only holds good in its application to individual cases ", should be abandoned in favour of a fluid conception of cause and effect as two things which are at the same time themselves and each other. Even if it were advisable, it is obviously impossible to think with such concepts, and nobody ever did so think, from Heraclitus to Lenin. But because Hegel called real thinking " metaphysical ", and adopted this clever name of *dialectic* for his perfectly metaphysical emotional communion with Absolute Change—which is related to real thinking just as a rotten spot is related to an apple—Marx and Engels, and every orthodox disciple of their science, including Lenin himself, has been induced to *believe* that he thinks with concepts each of which logically includes its opposite.

The real inference to be drawn from the fact that our thoughts do not give us " an exact representation of the universe ", is that we should cease putting up the pretence that they do. We should frankly acknowledge the instrumental character of all concepts, and face the fact that whatever generality and durability certain ones may attain, the only thing they can ultimately be relied upon to do is to solve specific problems. Knowledge is a thing to be found in practical good sense, and in the various sciences, and nowhere else. Not only is there no such thing as dialectic thinking, but there is no such super-intellectual knowledge of " the exact nature of the universe " as that to which an alleged dialectic thinking pretends to give access. You can discover realities, and experience them, and convey these experiences enriched and vivified in poetry, and you can define realities and interpret them for purposes of adjustment in practical language. You can mix poetry with practical language to make it lovable or persuasive. Beyond this you have the super-logical self-deception and nobly arduous nonsense of the metaphysicians, which makes you work harder, but has no other motive and no other practical significance than the sub-logical and simple nonsense of the professors of occultism. Neither of them has any place in a science of revolution.

People who are the most realistic in all other spheres, are just the ones most easily led away by myths in the sphere of psychology. It is because they are not introspective, and do not take any psychological statements as real statements of fact. It never occurs to them that a description of the process of thought is, or ought to be, just as specific and definite and subject to concrete verification as a description of the process of digestion. It would never occur to Lenin, for instance, that a good way to find out how a Marxian thinks, is to set a Marxian down at a table and let him honestly describe the process by which he reached some simple conclusion. And a way to verify what you learn by that experiment, is to set another Marxian down at another table, and let him describe the process by which he reached another conclusion. After about two hours expended in that merely preliminary scientific fashion, the whole myth about negating negations, and seeking in everything for its opposite, and never resting in an affirmative statement, and studying everything in its logical self-movement, its inner hostility against itself, and remembering that things can be both themselves and their opposites, and that cause and effect merge into each other, and that quantity becomes quality, and that nature makes jumps— this whole mixture of scientific commonplace with Hegelian higher-logical buncombe, which is being poured out by the centres of communist education in Russia

under the guise of instruction in the art of thinking—
would go up in the air and be forgotten forever. If
quantities become qualities, or if nature makes jumps,
that is a statement of fact, and it has no more bearing
upon the art of thinking than any other statement of fact.
The task of thinking is to determine, if possible, just
when and just where these specific events and others are
likely to occur, and how they can be made to occur.
And there is not a word of indication in all the literature
that has been spread abroad on this subject of dialectic
method, as to how that task can be fulfilled. Psychology is
indeed an infant science, but it has enough power of fact
in it to destroy this overgrown and fantastic mythology,
and it ought to be made a compulsory subject of study
for every Marxian.

The fact that Lenin did believe in " dialectic thinking "
will seem to many readers to disprove everything that
I say. Lenin was perhaps the most effective political
thinker in history, and he was one of the most adroit.
And Lenin believed that his thinking was " dialectic " ;
he cultivated his mind in the shadow of this belief. There
must be some value in dialectic thinking, then, besides
ceremonial communion with a God of change. And
indeed there is a value—not in dialectic thinking, for
that does not exist—but in *believing that you think dialectically*. And this value, instead of being in conflict
with what I have said, is exactly the proof of it. Believing
in dialectic thinking is a method by which having made
false intellectualistic assumptions about the nature of
thought, you can escape from them, and win back your
freedom to use thought as it was meant to be used.
If you know in the first place that thought is purposive,
and that logical concepts and all fixed principles are but
the instruments of action, then you are free to think

practically in a changing situation. You are free from
the domination of fixed ideas. You know that purpose
alone should dominate, and that ideas must always give
way before facts, you know that you must continually
recur to the facts, and be ready to remodel your ideas
to meet any unanticipated factual development. You
know that the more " theoretical " your ideas are—the
farther removed, that is, from mere statements of concrete
fact—the more purely their truth consists in the success
of their practical application. And since practical application must always be concrete and specific, you know
that truth is concrete and specific. All general statements,
and statements of what is true " in the abstract ", are
subject to suspicion. In short there are no fixed points
in thought, besides the beginning and the end of thinking,
and there is no possibility that thought, conceived as an
instrument of specific purposes, can ever arrive at anything more " absolute " than the statement of concrete facts.

All these things you will understand and assume,
without the aid of any mythology, if you know that thought
is a purposive function. But if you imagine that thought
is a purely intellectual reflection of reality, and that
logical ideas are automatic pictures of fact, then there
is only one way to get free from the domination of the
fixed meaning of those ideas. There is only one way
to justify yourself in changing them, and subordinating
them to your purpose and to the facts in a changing
situation. And that is to declare that it is the logical
nature of those ideas themselves to change. That is
what Lenin did. The " dialectic method " with Lenin
was simply a declaration of independence from the
domination of fixed concepts. It was a metaphysical
contraption by which he managed to defend his right
to use thoughts naturally, in spite of an unnatural conception of what thoughts are.

This may be proven, not only by examining the actual manner in which Lenin used thoughts, but by examining what he said about the dialectic itself. It is obvious that if dialectic thinking is what it pretends to be—a thinking with the self-contradictory concepts of the Hegelian speculative logic—then the first point to emphasize in teaching somebody to do it, is universal self-contradiction and the negation of the negation. And it is noticeable that Lenin, in the one passage in which he really undertook to explain what the dialectic is, not only did not mention this obviously preliminary point first, but he did not mention it at all. There is just one single idea in Lenin's statement of what " dialectic logic demands ", which distinctly and exclusively recalls Hegel's logic. Lenin says first, that we must not imagine that any one definition of an object exhausts its nature. A tumbler, for instance, may be defined as a glass cylinder, a thing to drink from, a prison for butterflies, and in many other ways. It is the same way with a labour union. We must study " all sides " of a thing, and " all its connections ". Second, we must study a thing in its change and development—and here he adds in quotation marks the word " self-movement ", which is Hegelian-metaphysical. Third, " all human practice must enter into our full definition of a thing, both as criterion of truth, and as practical determiner of its connection with what is needful to mankind ". And fourth, " dialectic logic teaches that ' there is no abstract truth, truth is always concrete ' ".

That is the whole of Lenin's explicit instruction to his followers in the art of dialectic thinking. It was given at a moment when the question which of two groups was thinking dialectically, and which " scholastically ", had been raised in connection with a critical problem in Soviet politics. And although Lenin added that " he

did not of course exhaust the concept of dialectic logic ",
it is certain that he stated what its essential practical
meaning was to him. And if you wish to see that meaning
summed up in one word, you have it here, in one of his
last attacks upon the leaders of the Second International :

"They call themselves Marxists, but understand Marxism
to an impossible degree pedantically. The decisive thing in
Marxism they completely fail to understand, namely, its
revolutionary dialectic. Even the direct statement of Marx
that revolutionary moments demand a maximum of flexibility, is unintelligible to them. . . ."

That is what " dialectic thinking " meant to Lenin.
It meant *flexibility*—a maximum of flexibility, as opposed
to the " pedantry " of ordinary intellectualism. It meant
that ideas should be handled as instruments of action,
and not actions mechanically deduced from ideas. Every
one of the four demands of " dialectic logic ", according
to Lenin, is a simple application of the essence of the
functional view of intelligence. And not one of them
gives a hint of the essence of the Hegelian logic.

As we have seen, Marxism has been a perpetual struggle
between metaphysical presuppositions and practical
revolutionary realism. Lenin's wisdom was simply
the highest development of that practical realism. And
his forgetting about the law of self-contradiction was
an indispensable part of his wisdom. For that " law "
is not only superfluous, but it is hostile, to the achievement
of flexibility. It is a perfect example of one of those
pretended abstract truths, which make impossible the
concrete adjustment of ideas to the moving variety of
facts. Marx did not succeed in forgetting this " abstract
truth " as well as Lenin did, but even he managed to
keep it usually out of the way of his practical thinking.
And when it came to summarizing the dialectic in a

word, he said the same thing that Lenin did. He described it as a " free movement " of the mind in the " empirical material ". Engels too declared that " the kernel of the dialectic view " is a knowledge that nature is fluid, and that " fixity and absoluteness are the products of our own minds ". Plekhanov said that " the search for concrete truth constitutes the distinguishing feature of dialectic thinking "—which is but another way of saying *flexibility*, and *freedom of movement in the empirical material*, for it is only " abstract truths " which deprive us of this freedom.

All these statements by great Marxists of what seems to them the essential factor in the dialectic method, ignore what must obviously be the essential factor of thinking based upon Hegel's logic. They all point directly to the essential factor in thinking which understands its origin, and is consciously purposive. Practical Marxists have merely used the idea of this mysterious logic, in order to gain the freedom to think purposively in spite of their education. It has been a way out of intellectualistic presuppositions into the world of practical action. With Hegel it was a way out of these same presuppositions into a world of metaphysical emotion. Abandon those intellectualistic presuppositions, and you destroy both of these " ways out ". But you find yourself *in* the world of practical action, for that is the real world in which the function of thinking actually developed.

PART II

THE SCIENCE OF REVOLUTIONARY ENGINEERING

CHAPTER I

MARXISM AS A SCIENCE

THE motion of thought, in its origin and main development, is a motion back and forth and round about among given facts, desired ends, and plans of action for achieving the ends upon the basis of the facts. When thinking becomes very abstract and is cultivated for its own sake, or when an attempt is made to state the nature of certain facts independently of their relation to any specific end, this natural process is considerably changed, and a number of difficult problems about it arise. But these problems do not arise in connection with any thinking, no matter how " theoretical ", which is concerned with the concrete practical problems of human life. Such thinking always conforms, whether consciously and with exactitude or not, to the instrumental pattern. The emphasis in any given case may be upon an accurate definition of the factual situation—but even here the end will show its influence in the facts selected and the manner of their formulation. Or the emphasis may be upon a delineation of the end, or ideal—though here still more obviously the existing facts will appear. And if the emphasis is upon a precision of the hypothesis, or plan of action, still the situation must be designated in which it is to be applied, and the end must be defined in order to put it to the test of action. These three elements are all united compactly in perception, and practical thought only separates them tentatively and imperfectly, and for the purpose of uniting them again.

Marxism, liberated from the metaphysical frame in which Marx tried to confine it, can be very easily restated in the form of a practical science. It was created by combining three intellectual disciplines : that of the classical economists, who had occupied themselves with a definition of the existing mechanism of human society ; that of the utopian socialists who had put their emphasis upon the delineation of an ideal society ; and that of the young Hegelians who were absorbed in the idea of historic process. Marxism as a practical science redefines the existing mechanism of society from the standpoint of the ends proposed by the utopian socialists ; it redefines those ends from the standpoint of the facts of economics ; and it points out the method of procedure by which it will be possible to take a real step from the existing situation in the direction of the desired ends.

Marx saw, to begin with, that economics does define the essential mechanism of human society. This society is predominantly neither a political nor a " civil " gathering, but a business association ; and the major forces which control its operation are economic class-interests. Anyone who wants to change any human society fundamentally must attack its economic structure, and he must work with these economic forces. Approaching with this wisdom the society of our own day, Marx identified the two facts of essential importance for those who want to change it in the direction suggested by the utopians—the fact that the production of wealth is becoming more and more co-operative, and the fact that the control of this process is becoming more and more centralized, and concentrated in the hands of a small class. He saw that both these tendencies would increase with the further invention of machinery. He concluded that the only practical revolutionary plan for our day, is to transfer this centralized control of the co-operative process of production into the hands of the producers collectively organized. And he saw further that the only force capable of accomplishing this change is the revolutionary self-interest of the producers themselves, the wage-working class. The Marxian method is to accentuate the class struggle between workers and capitalists, organize it both nationally and internationally, and carry it forward, undeceived by political forms and ideologies, and in full consciousness of the ruthlessness of the forces in play, to the goal of a revolutionary dictatorship of the proletariat. Such a dictatorship could actually expropriate the owners of the land and the instruments of labour, and reduce them to the position of equal participators in the social process of production. That fundamental step having been taken, human society could begin to move in the direction of freedom, and political sincerity, and international peace, and an opportunity of life for every member of it. . . . That is what Marxism is, in outline, in so far as it is a concrete science of revolution, and not an abstract philosophy of the universe.

Having been formulated as a system of historic metaphysics, this practical science is naturally imperfect and incomplete. It particularly needs supplementing with an investigation and formulation, from the point of view of the revolutionary purpose, of the facts of human nature. It needs verification and guidance from the science of psychology. And that is the same thing as saying that it needs to become more concrete. For there is no other opposition between Marxism *as a science* and the science of psychology, except that the one is a broad generalization and the other a detailed investigation. They contemplate the same facts, and their view of these facts is in profound harmony. Not only does the psychology of Freud bear out in a startling way Marx's generalization about past history, but the conception of the hereditary nature of man which prevails among biological and experimental psychologists confirms unconditionally Marx's rejection of utopian-evangelical methods for producing in the future an industrially democratic commonwealth. It is possible for a psychologist who is scientific to deny the possibility of producing such a commonwealth, but it would be hard for him to deny that the method of class struggle and proletarian dictatorship is the only method yet proposed which takes into consideration the facts of human nature. Instead of being afraid of psychology, as the Marxian philosophers are, a Marxian scientist would embrace it with enthusiasm as offering a final and more cogent, because more factually analytical, confirmation of his general plan of work.

It is not the present business to outline the science of human behaviour as it relates to the revolutionary purpose. But one thing at least may be stated, because it flows from the very terms in which the problem arises. Such a science will make a clear and vital distinction between the general mass of mankind in society, and those individuals who have risen above their own social position in order to understand society as a whole, and devote themselves to an effort to improve it. It will put a new emphasis upon the separate identity and unusual motivation of the revolutionary scientist himself. It will make no effort to conceal the peculiar relation in which he stands to the human material with which he works. Marx himself recognized this distinction in the early days before the dialectic metaphysics had crystallized in his mind.

"The materialistic teaching," he wrote, " that men are a product of environment and education—changed men, therefore, the product of other environment and changed education—forgets that the environment is changed by men, and that the educator himself has to be educated. It becomes necessary, therefore, to divide society into two parts of which the one is elevated above society." . . . And to this, in order to make the meaning unmistakable, Engels added in parenthesis the words " Robert Owen ".

If this " division of society " had been kept in mind by Marx and Engels, and made as much of as the division of society into proletariat and bourgeoisie, scientific socialism would have a very different aspect from what it has. Instead of being described as " a union of science with the proletariat ", it would be described as a union of scientists, or of scientific idealists—who may or may not be of proletarian origin—with the proletariat. Such a description is true to the human facts, or will be true to them, at least, when socialism really becomes a science. And it will inevitably come to the front as soon as a chapter on human nature is embodied in a practical text-book of revolution.

In order to teach the science of revolution to a mind uncorrupted by metaphysics, one should begin, it seems to me, with an outline of the idea of a true society, as it has been developed by the great utopians all the way from Plato to Kropotkin. Everyone who is alive enough to be educated will have a certain interest in that idea. And then one should explain that these utopians, although their idea was not unreasonable, were impractical in their attitude toward it. For, proposing the most gigantic undertaking conceivable on this earth, they devoted the main part of their thoughts to describing what an improvement the result would be, and how reasonable and beautiful it was. A gigantic practical undertaking demands first an examination of the existing materials and forces, and the formation upon the basis of this examination of a plan for achieving it. It is this examination and definition of fact, with a view to achieving an otherwise utopian idea, which constitutes the essential scientific work of Karl Marx. His plan can be shown to grow inevitably out of an adequate comprehension and bold facing of the facts. It is the only plan yet proposed which these facts do not clearly prove to be impractical. . . .

In this way Marxism could be taught without mysticism, and without pretending that human thought is something else besides what it is. The teaching would have a different emphasis according as the student himself were a member of the working class, or of the propertied intelligentsia, but it would not differ in its essential simple character of pointing the way out of a situation that is unsatisfactory.

CHAPTER II

THE ANARCHIST CONTRIBUTION

SCIENTIFIC procedure has to be distinguished, not only from religious ceremony, but also from magic, from all the relics of the profane practice of the Medicine Man—alchemy, astrology, and so forth. The distinction here is not one of emotional motive or general mental attitude, for both the magician and the scientist attempt to change, or adjust themselves to, a world which they conceive as impersonal. The distinction lies in their attitude to the unchangeable or uncontrollable element in that world. The magician ignores this element, or reduces it in his imagination to a negligible minimum. The desired end plays the predominant part in his thinking, the given facts play almost no part at all. The scientist not only pays attention to those given facts, but he spends the best of his time ascertaining their exact character and defining them. His effort to change and control the world is based upon and guided by a definition of what is unchangeable or uncontrollable about it. Thus, for example, the alchemists of the Middle Ages attempted by every sort of random device to convert various substances into gold, but they did not examine the interior structure of these substances or the laws of their behaviour. The science of chemistry was born when Robert Boyle turned his attention exclusively to determining that interior structure and those laws. But the original purpose was in principle only postponed ; the science of chemistry may yet succeed, it seems, in converting other substances into gold.

Now Marxism—in so far as it is a science, and not a philosophy—bears substantially the same relation to the efforts of utopian-evangelical reformers, that chemistry does to the efforts of alchemists. It defines the structure of human society and determines the forces which control it, and upon the basis of those given facts which are not changeable, it proposes a method by which human society can be changed. Revolutionary anarchism, on the contrary, clings to the attitude of the alchemists, and the utopians. It merely adds the mystic act of insurrection against government to the spells of reasonable eloquence, that were supposed to " call up " the ideal society. The relation of anarchists to a real science of revolution is the same as that of amateur " healers "— the survivors of wizardry—to the science of medicine. They survive by refusing to acknowledge, or concentrate their attention upon, the unchangeable or uncontrollable elements in the given facts, to formulate these elements in " laws ", and thus arrive at a systematic procedure by which the given facts can be actually and not only imaginatively changed or controlled. The procedure of the revolutionary anarchist, generally speaking, is to dwell upon the idea of a true society, and assist at moments of crisis in destroying the existing order, in the faith that this idea will be realized. That this is not the procedure of practical science is obvious, and it could be explained very simply and convincingly by Marxists, if Marxism itself were a practical science.

But since the practical science in Marxism was misborn and crippled to fit the forms of a metaphysical religion, its relation to anarchism is by no means so simple. There are certain respects in which Marxism is the less scientific of the two. It is less scientific in its attitude toward the goal of revolutionary effort. Just as the anarchists, in their preoccupation with the goal, fail to consider the facts and the method of procedure, so the Marxists in their apotheosis of the facts and the method, fail to consider the goal. It was possible for Marx, under the guise of a " philosophy of history ", to define the relevant facts ; and in the dress of " historic necessity " it was possible to present a plan of action. But Marx's religion offered no device by which he could adequately investigate the third problem essential to a scientific procedure, the problem of the possibility and appropriateness of the ideal, or objective end, of the undertaking. Instead of examining and redefining this ideal in the light of his definition of the facts, Marx merely ceased to talk about it. His dialectic religion assured him that the " contradictions " in capitalism must inevitably be " resolved " by an expropriation of the capitalists, and a collective ownership of the means of production. It also declared that the state, which had arisen out of these contradictions, would " die away " after they were resolved. This was sufficient for a preliminary definition of his purpose— a determination of the general direction of activities at least up to the conquest of power. And any remaining questions Marx answered by tacking on to these two conceptions, in a very undialectic and irresponsible manner, the most utopian of all the formulæ for the millennium : " From each according to his abilities, to each according to his needs." That is the extent of the Marxian science, so far as concerns drawing up a prospectus, or ground plan, of the thing to be achieved.

It was quite inevitable that Marx, imagining his own plan of action to be a description of what history was about to do, should thus leave to " history " the lion's share of the worry about the end to be arrived at. And it was inevitable that his followers, imagining Marx's metaphysical personification of history to be a materialistic science, should resist as " unscientific " every impulse of simple and sensible-minded people to make some inquiries about it.

"What is the value henceforth," says Plekhanov, "of those more or less laborious and more or less ingenious researches as to the best possible form of social organization ? None, literally none ! They can only testify to the lack of scientific instruction of those who enter upon them. Their day is past forever."

If Plekhanov had been a practical man, he could not have failed to see that if there is no need of defining the goal of your efforts, there is no need of guiding them. If the economic God is taking care of the remote future, must He not take care of to-morrow ? And if not, then at what point in the unbroken flow of events, does your jurisdiction end, and that of the economic God begin ? A practical engineer could not fail to ask this question, for the simple reason that until it was answered he could not complete his plans—which reveals again the incompatibility of all philosophies of absolute determinism with all practical science.

The fact is that a definition of the goal of revolutionary effort, while it must remain, during the early stages of the undertaking, abstract and free and subject to radical redefinition, is nevertheless indispensable to scientific procedure. Without investigating at least the abstract possibility of the society aimed at, its compatibility with the hereditary instincts of man, and thus the probability of its enduring if it were once established, no maturely scientific person would devote himself to the effort. The utopian socialists had begun such an investigation, and in abandoning it Marxism took a step backward from utopian socialism. The anarchists have continued this investigation, and that constitutes their chief contribution to the science of revolution.

" The question put by anarchism," says Kropotkin, " might be expressed in the following way : ' Which social forms best guarantee in such and such societies, and in humanity at large, the greatest sum of happiness and therefore the greatest sum of vitality ? ' ' Which forms of society are most likely to allow this sum of happiness to increase and develop in quantity and quality—that is to say, will enable this happiness to become more complete and more varied ? ' "

Kropotkin brought a vast body of biological and historical data to bear upon this important—and in a proper scientific procedure, preliminary—question. His book " Mutual Aid " is of the highest revolutionary-scientific importance. He neglected, or refused to see, the relevance to his problem of the data supplied by Marx in his study of modern capitalism. And like all modern revolutionary writers he ignored the contributions of psychology. For these reasons his writings are inadequate and in need of revision. But they remain, both in their attitude and their information upon the question of the goal of revolutionary effort, a long stride in advance of Marxism.

Another matter in which the anarchists are in advance of the Marxists, is their conscious renunciation of metaphysics, their unfulfilled, but real aspiration toward a practical scientific attitude. Bakunin's early protest against the " everlasting theoretical insanity " of Karl Marx, runs through all the great anarchist literature, and it is essentially wise and just. It is the protest of all simple minds, with a healthy love for clarity and directness, against tangling up the real act of revolution in the unreal and awful ponderosities of German metaphysics.

Bakunin himself did not entirely escape from that theoretical insanity which he despised ; he wrote his share of Hegelian higher nonsense. And Proudhon, the other founder of modern anarchism, was only saved from it by his ignorance. Nevertheless they both represent in their conflict with Marx, the tendency toward a more direct and natural use of the practical function of intelligence. Marx's famous attack upon the philosophic pretences of Proudhon is a pitiless exposure of the philosophic infirmities of Marx.

" Let us see now," he says, " the modification to which Herr Proudhon subjects the dialectic of Hegel in applying it to political economy. For Herr Proudhon, every economic category has two sides, a good and a bad . . .
" The *good side* and the *bad side*, the *advantage* and the *disadvantage* taken together, constitute for Herr Proudhon the *contradiction* in each economic category.
" The problem to solve : to conserve the good side, and eliminate the bad. . . .
" Hegel has no problems to put. He knows only the dialectic. Herr Proudhon has of the Hegelian dialectic nothing but the phraseology. His own dialectic method consists in the dogmatic distinction of good and evil.
" Let us for an instant take Herr Proudhon himself as a category. Let us examine his good and his bad side, his advantages and his disadvantages . . ."

Marx is amusing in this polemic, and he successfully convicts Herr Proudhon of bombastic pretentiousness and a complete ignorance of philosophy. But ignorance of philosophy is a kind of wisdom. And it is certain that in the above passage Proudhon's *naïveté* is both wiser and more scientific than Marx's sophistication. Marx gave his life to an attempt to solve the problem, how " to preserve the good side while eliminating the bad side " of modern capitalism. That is the simple fact. And a person who understands psychological facts can only smile at the sophomoric assurance with which Marx asserts what he had learned at school to the contrary. Marx was not defending science here against the sentimentality of Herr Proudhon. He was defending a metaphysical rationalization of his motives, against that simple recognition and definition of them, which might have been the foundation of a concrete science.

Thus Proudhon's ignorance played the same part as Bakunin's impatience. It gave to anarchism a tendency away from metaphysics, and made it seem more practical and more convincing to many clear and scientific minds, than Marxism. And Peter Kropotkin, himself a man of science, raised this wise tendency in his predecessors to a conscious article of faith. He rejected both the academic and the Marxian economics on the ground that they were deductive and metaphysical and ignorant of the methods of applied science. There is nothing wiser in revolutionary literature than what he wrote on this subject.

" It is possible," he concluded, " that we are wrong, and they [the Marxists] are right. But the question which of us is right, and which wrong, cannot be settled by means of Byzantine commentaries as to what such and such a writer intended to say, or by talking about what agrees with the ' trilogy ' of Hegel ; most certainly not by continuing to use the dialectic method.

" It can be done only by studying the facts of economics in the same way and by the same methods as we study the natural sciences . . .

" There is one point upon which without doubt anarchism is absolutely in the right. It is when it . . . parts forever with metaphysics."

In spite of this admirable and unanswerable declaration, Kropotkin did not employ the methods of applied science upon the problem of producing an anarchist-communist society. Having investigated the question, *What social forms would guarantee to humanity the greatest sum of happiness and vitality ?* he did not turn round and examine the existing social forms with a view to answering the question, *What social procedure will actually move us from the one situation in the direction of the other ?*

Having asked, and to the best of his ability answered, that preliminary question, he abandoned the methods of applied science altogether, and adopted in its place two contrary attitudes, between which he shifted back and forth in a way that serves only the purposes of intellectual confusion.

One of his attitudes was an ineffectual pretence at " pure " science. That is to say, he objectively *predicted* the anarchist-communist society on the basis of " tendencies " which he professed to discover in biology and human history. It is needless to say that in proving the predominance of these " tendencies ", he did not employ those methods of accurate definition, and real verification, which he advocated so eloquently in his attack upon Marxism. Kropotkin's assertion on " inductive " grounds of the inevitability of the communist society, has no more scientific validity, than the Marxian assertion of the same thing on the ground of Hegelian Logic.

His other attitude was in the broad sense " practical ", but it was no less utopian than that of his predecessors. It consisted of advocating evangelical miracles, and relying upon a magic supposed to reside in the mere act of revolution, to accomplish the transformation which he desired.

" For the triumph of the revolution, men must first get rid of their faith in Law, Authority, Unity, Order, Property, and other institutions inherited from past times when our forefathers were slaves.

" Without such [insurrectionary] risings, the social mind was never able to get rid of its deep-rooted prejudices. . . .

" The lessons of history tell us that a new form of economic life always calls forth a new form of political organization . . . Consequently the chief aim of anarchism is to awaken those constructive powers of the labouring masses of the people which at all great moments of history come forward to accomplish the necessary changes. . . ."

These quotations are sufficient to show that Kropotkin did not succeed, any more than the other anarchists, in substituting the methods of applied science for Marx's metaphysical approach to the social problem. The method of revolutionary anarchism, speaking broadly and yet with technical accuracy, is to conjure up the communist society by the magical act of revolution.

This does not prevent a certain co-operation between anarchists and scientific revolutionists in times of propaganda or preparation. But in a revolutionary crisis, the scientific procedure by which alone the forces in revolt can be made to produce a preliminary result in the desired direction—the proletarian dictatorship—seems to the anarchist to be the very obstacle preventing the complete magical transformation which he had anticipated. The more naïvely sincere is his faith in that magical transformation, the more surely will he put himself in opposition to the scientific movement. He will become a counter-revolutionary force, and to the extent practically necessary must be unhesitatingly so dealt with by those who are trying to do something in real fact, and not only in emotional imagination.

CHAPTER III

REVOLUTIONARY SYNDICALISM

REVOLUTIONARY syndicalism contributed to the attempt to define an ideal society a conception of the dominating rôle which might be played by the labour unions—a conception which will certainly not be passed over by a mature science of revolution. It also contributed to revolutionary method a sense of the danger involved in political activities, the necessity of unusual honesty in leaders, and the necessity of emphasizing the class character of the revolution. But syndicalism did not escape from the utopian mode of thought of the anarchists to whom it owes its origin. Like them it solved the problem presented by the enormous complexity and inevitable centralization of modern production, by refusing to face it—by " believing in " decentralization. It solved the problem of the existing state by wishing it away. It solved the problem of the future state by attributing to the labour unions some mysterious property which will enable them to rule without being a government. And to the idea of a General Strike it attributed occult powers of an altogether unimagined potency. The General Strike, according to some of the syndicalist writers, will not only conjure away the existing state, and the centralization of modern industry, and transfer the direction of society to the individual labour unions, but it will regenerate man in a moral sense, and fill him with a permanent enthusiasm like that possessed by the soldiers of the French Revolution.

It is impossible not to see in this total want of proportion between cause and effect a survival of the conjuror's faith in a ritual performance.

Revolutionary syndicalism made utopian thinking seem more plausible to practical minds by associating it with references to actually existing working-class organizations, and by emphasizing the principal action which these organizations will naturally take in a revolutionary crisis.   But as a practical method for revolutionizing society, it did not take one solid step away from that belief in magic, which characterizes the attitude of the anarchists.[1]

On the other hand, the syndicalists took a great step backward from the anarchist position by producing a metaphysician and adding to their utopian beginnings of science all the essential faults of animistic thinking. In the writings of George Sorel every point in which anarchism was genuinely in advance of Marxism, is explicitly relinquished.   The sane determination of the anarchists to discuss the possibility of a more ideal society, and the form which it ought to take, is renounced in favour of a mystic abandonment to the élan of the present moment.

" One must not hope," says Sorel, " that the revolutionary movement can ever follow a direction conveniently deter-

---

[1] The Industrial Workers of the World have a more businesslike way of talking than some of the European syndicalists, but the motto which they substitute for the Marxian plan of political dictatorship—" Build the new society within the shell of the old "—shows a similar disregard of the practical terms of the problem.   It shows the same reliance upon magical transformations—reliance indeed upon a metaphor—to solve the essential problem of the transference of power.

The " Syndicalist-Communist " group now surrounding Pierre Monatte in France occupies a peculiar position, not yet clearly formulated, it seems to me, and expressly omitted from this discussion.

mined in advance, that it can be conducted according to a learned plan like the conquest of a country, that it can be studied scientifically otherwise than in its present. Everything in it is unpredictable."

The determination of the anarchists to be simple and intelligible, to have done with learned obscurities and the solemn casuistries of the " short-coated priests " of philosophy, is likewise abandoned by Sorel. For him the inextricable tangle of animism and science which makes Marxism fundamentally unintelligible to clear-minded people who are honest enough to say so, is the primary virtue of Marxism.

" Socialism is necessarily a very obscure matter," he tells us, " since it treats of production, that is to say of that which is most mysterious in human activity, and since it proposes to bring a radical transformation into this region which it is impossible to describe with the clarity which one finds in superficial regions of the world. No effort of thought, no progress of knowledge, no reasonable induction can ever dispel the mystery which envelops socialism ; and it is because Marxism has well recognized this character that it has won the right to serve as the point of departure for socialist studies."

The manner in which Sorel managed to introduce into an anarchist movement all the essential faults of Marxism was comparatively simple. The anarchists had got rid of Hegel ; they had freed their minds of the father-fixation upon a conservative professor of religious and patriotic metaphysics. Sorel could not go back to Hegel ; that would have been obviously reactionary. But he discovered in his own times another conservative professor of patriotism and religious metaphysics, Henri Bergson. He attached the anarcho-syndicalist proposal to the animism of this new philosopher, and thus gave a progressive appearance to the longest backward step yet taken by any genuinely revolutionary theorist.

In place of the dialectic evolution of a determined universe in the direction of our heart's desire, Sorel gives us the " creative evolution " of a free universe in the same general direction. In place of the historic necessity of the social revolution, he gives us the *indispensability to evolution* of the social myth of the revolution. In place of the worship of dialectic, the scorn of " scientism ". In place of the Hegelian-Marxian higher logic, in which " the life-process of the material receives its mental reflection ", he gives us the Bergsonian vital intuition, another superior kind of intelligence in which " reason, hopes, and the perception of the particular facts seem to make but one indivisible unity ". In short he gets his own purpose transplanted into the facts, and substitutes emotional co-operation with the objective world, for the attempt to make something out of it. To preserve this religious attitude in spite of the advance of science, is the dominating motive of Bergson's philosophy, just as it was the dominating motive of Hegel's. That is why Sorel could substitute Bergson for Hegel, and yet arrive at a position not radically contrasted with metaphysical Marxism.

It is highly desirable to reconcile anarcho-syndicalism with Marxism—or rather to reconcile anarchists and syndicalists to the practical science that is concealed in Marxism. But it will not be accomplished by abandoning all the virtues of anarchism and embracing all the faults of Marxism. It will be accomplished by recognizing that each has over-emphasized one part of a complete act of practical intelligence to the neglect of the other part. The anarchists have neglected to define the unalterable element in the facts, and formulate the method of procedure compatible with its continued existence. The Marxists have neglected to define the ideal, and bring it into working relation with their definition of fact and their method of procedure. The fault in Marxism is far less serious, at least in the early stages of the undertaking, because the general direction of revolutionary effort, the outline of its ideal, is commonly agreed upon and can be taken for granted. Moreover, in recognizing and resolutely facing an unalterable element in the facts, Marxism took that one step on the road to scientific method which is the most difficult for idealistic minds to take. And under cover of its legend of dialectic thinking, Marxism unconsciously anticipated a more advanced conception of intelligence, and a more scientific employment of it, than was known to those anarchists who attacked this legend in the name of science. For these reasons, in spite of its surreptitious preservation of the animistic attitude, Marxism and not anarchism laid the foundation for a practical science of revolution.

CHAPTER IV

BOLSHEVISM

IF you wanted to build a bridge across a stream, it would be absurd to make your calculations upon the assumption that the properties of steel and iron are such that they are going across the stream, and that you are lending consciousness to the process. It would not require a book to demonstrate that this was a relic of animism. In creating a dictatorship of the proletariat, as a bridge toward a real human society, the absurdity of this way of calculating is less obvious, but it is equally great. The only difference here is that the material you work with is moving, and it is human, and you are a part of it. This does not alter the nature of thought and purposive action, or justify you in regarding yourself as a reflecting apparatus, instead of an engineer. It merely gives rise to a large and altogether peculiar set of engineering problems. And it was exactly these problems which Lenin solved, and whose solution created the " Bolshevik " departure in Marxism. Lenin's fundamental contribution to the Marxian science was a determination of the way in which engineers who use it, must relate themselves to the moving human material of which they are a part.

Bolshevism, like so many other things, can be best understood by studying it at the point of origin. It was born in Lenin's attack upon a school of compromising Marxists who called themselves " Economists ". Their idea was that the Marxian intellectuals in Russia ought not to alienate the workers by stressing the political aspect of the revolution, the necessity of overthrowing the czar's government, but ought simply to enter into the economic struggle with the bosses, leaving these political changes to follow in the natural course of events. They ought to subordinate themselves to the spontaneous, or as they called it " elemental ", movement of the workers. Lenin destroyed this humble-casuistical tendency completely in his journal " Iskra " and his book " What to Do ? " He put in its place the idea of an " organization of professional revolutionists ", who, while welding themselves into a dynamic identity with the elemental movement of the workers, should nevertheless retain their own organizational identity, and their own intellectual identity—their unqualified and undissembled loyalty to the whole programme of political and economic revolution. He maintained that such an organization was not only advisable, but indispensable to victory. " I assert," he said, " that no revolutionary movement can be durable without a solid organization of leaders capable of maintaining their succession."

In his further development and the development of his party, Lenin ceased to employ the concept of " professional revolutionist ". It was a peculiarly Russian concept—the essential fruit, indeed, of that consecrated movement of revolt which had preceded Bolshevism in Russia. And Lenin apparently knew that it was Russian. He knew that it was out of accord with the Marxian manner of thinking as it had developed in western Europe. He always resisted the proposal to translate into other languages the book in which he had laid down the foundations of Bolshevism. But he never yielded to those in Russia who accused him of having exaggerated in that book the rôle of these " professional revolutionists ". He replied that their rôle *had been* indispensable, and he explained the disappearance of this concept from his writings of a later date, by saying that the " professional revolutionist has done his work in the history of Russian proletarian socialism ". He has succeeded, that is, in welding himself into a dynamic unity with the elemental struggle of the workers, so that the organization ultimately formed can be treated as a single unit, the " vanguard " of the revolutionary proletariat. By an adroit use of this word " vanguard ", Lenin reconciled his language in later years with that of western European Marxism. But I believe no Bolshevik would deny that the professional revolutionist continued, during the growth and triumph of Lenin's party, to play the same indispensable rôle that was ascribed to him at its foundation. In the official " History of the Russian Communist Party," published during Lenin's life, we read :

" If you inquire, from the standpoint of the personal staff of leaders, what our party lives by at the present time, and even our state, it will become clear that to a significant degree even now after twenty years, the party so to speak, nourishes itself upon that group of professional revolutionists, the foundations of which were laid at the beginning of the century."

The concept of professional revolutionist belongs, then, not only to the origin, but to the essence of Bolshevism. And if you will reflect how directly a person's " class " depends upon his " profession ", you will see that to make revolution itself a " profession ",. was a very real departure in a philosophy which regards revolution as an automatic outcome of the struggle of classes. To declare that the people of that " profession " are indispensable to the victory of the working class, has the appearance of heresy. And this appearance becomes more pronounced when you learn that, in describing his professional revolutionists, Lenin repeatedly declared that :" it makes no difference " whether they belong to the working class or not.

"The organization of revolutionists," he said, " ought to embrace first of all and chiefly people whose profession consists of revolutionary activity. . . . And before this general title of member of the organization, all distinction between workers and intelligentsia should be obliterated, to say nothing of distinctions between this and that separate profession."

Thus Lenin founded his Bolshevik organization upon a recognition of the *indispensable* historic function of a group of people who were not defined according to the economic class to which they belonged, but were defined according to their purposive activity and their state of mind. They were people committed and consecrated to a certain social purpose—but with this difference, from the " Narodniki ", that they possessed the Marxian science and the Marxian technique for the achievement of that purpose. In short, they were scientific revolu-tionary engineers.

Lenin was accused by other Marxists of " Jacobinism " and " Blanquism " on the ground of this heresy, and I think the accusation should have been accepted. Lenin was amazingly contented, or rather determined, to attribute all of his wisdom to Karl Marx. It seemed to fulfill some need of his emotional nature to do so. But a mature history of his policies would neglect neither his own contributions nor those of the great French revolutionists. Lenin corrected the error of Marx, which was a mystic faith in the proletariat as such ; and he corrected the error of Blanqui, which was to trust all to the organization of revolutionists. He saw that the organization of revolutionists must be actually rooted in, and welded together with, the proletariat by a whole series of personal and organizational bonds, so that they not only assume to represent the proletariat, but also, when a revolutionary period arrives, actually do represent it. But he saw also that they must be a distinct body of men who " stand above society ", and are thus able to understand it. And his arrant insistence upon centralized authority and military discipline in that body of men, smacks more of the tactics of Blanqui than of the philosophy of Marx.

Moreover, in discussing the part to be played by this organization of revolutionists, Lenin contradicted the Marxian metaphysics and abandoned it absolutely. He abandoned all the confused ideological dodges of the priest of economic metaphysics, who is " bringing to the working class a consciousness of its destiny ", and adopted the attitude of a practical artisan who is doing work, and doing it scientifically, and not seriously deceiving himself either about the historic destiny of his material, or the essentially decorative function of his own brain and volition. It is not easy to find a formula that will flatly and absolutely contradict an animistic construction as subtle as that invented by Hegel and stood on its head by Marx. But in this book " What to Do ? " Lenin succeeded in finding one. He denied both its assertion that the material elements of the world are automatically evolving towards socialism, and its assertion that the thoughts of socialists are a mere reflection of the process.

" The elemental development of the workers' movement," he said, " goes straight toward subjection to the bourgeois ideology . . . for the elemental workers' movement is trade-unionism . . . and trade-unionism means just exactly the intellectual enslavement of the workers by the bourgeoisie. For that reason our task, the task of the social-democracy consists in a *struggle with elementalness*, it consists in dragging the workers' movement away from its instinctive trade-union aspiration under the wing of the bourgeoisie, and attracting it under the wing of the social-democracy. The statement of the Economists, that no efforts even of the most inspired ideologists can distract the workers' movement from the path determined by the interaction of the material forces with the material means of production is equivalent to a renunciation of socialism. . . .

" There cannot develop among the workers a consciousness of the irreconcilable opposition of their interests to the whole contemporary political and social structure—that is, a socialist consciousness. . . . That can only be brought in from the outside. The history of all countries testifies that all by itself the working class is able to develop only a trade-union consciousness—a conviction of the necessity of combining in unions to carry on the struggle with the bosses, to extract from the Government this or that law indispensable to the workers, etc. . . . The science of socialism grew out of those philosophical, historical, and economic theories, which were developed by cultivated representatives of the possessing class. . . . This does not mean, of course, that working-men do not participate in the working out of those theories. But they participate not in the capacity of working-men, but in the capacity of socialist theorists, . . . participate, in short, only when and in so far as they have succeeded to a greater or less extent in mastering the science of their age and advancing it. . . .

" Without a revolutionary theory there can be no revolutionary movement. . . . The Economists accuse ' Iskra ' of ' setting its programme over against the workers' movement like a spirit soaring above formless chaos '. In what consists the rôle of the social-democracy, if not in being the ' spirit ', not only soaring above the elemental movement, but raising the latter up to its programme ? It certainly does not consist in dragging oneself along in the tail of the movement. . . . One must indeed confess that people firmly determined always to follow a movement in the capacity of the tail, are once and for all absolutely guaranteed against ' minimizing the elemental factor '. . . ."

It is obvious that this is not Hegelian Marxism. This is a series of violent and magnificent denials of the whole thing. For the substance of Hegelian Marxism is the assertion that the proletariat *as such*, and by virtue of a dialectic necessity inherent in its elemental and material nature, is bound to fight the bourgeoisie and achieve the revolution, and that ideas and theories in the minds of socialists can be nothing but a reflection of the process. This fact was pointed out in the Party Congress of 1903 by one of the " Economists ", Martinov, who arrayed against Lenin a whole series of contrary quotations from Marx and Engels, and from socialist programmes of other countries. But Lenin had then the support of Plekhanov. He had the majority of the Congress. He dismissed Martinov's theoretical attack with the remark that " the Economists had bent the stick in one direction, and in order to straighten the stick it was necessary to bend it in the other ". This was no answer at all, for there was no element of degree in Lenin's heresy. He had given to his super-class professional revolutionists, defined and identified by their purposive ideas and idealistic activities, an indispensable dynamic function in the historic process which Marx's Hegelian philosophy absolutely denies to them.

Plekhanov was aware of this fact, and he said so as soon as he had decided to abandon Lenin politically. He said that he had told Lenin his book was theoretically wrong when he saw it in manuscript. He said that he had " never regarded Lenin as an able theorist, and always considered him organically incapable of dialectic thinking ". He said that Lenin's popularity was due to a " departure from Marxism which made his ideas accessible to those 'practicals' who are unprepared to understand Marxism ". He proved this with a quotation from Marx :

" It is not a question of what goal this or that proletarian sets himself at a given time, or even the whole proletariat. It is a question of what the class is in itself, and of what, in view of this its being, it is historically bound to accomplish."

He reminded his readers that according to the philosophy of historic materialism, " Economic necessity gives birth to and carries to its logical end—that is, to the social revolution—that movement of the working class of which scientific socialism serves as a theoretic expression." And he excommunicated Lenin from the true church of this philosophy in these words :

" The disputed question consists in this : Does there exist an economic necessity which calls forth in the proletariat a demand for socialism, makes it instinctively socialistic, and impels it—even if left to its own resources—on the road to social revolution, notwithstanding the stubborn and continual effort of the bourgeoisie to subject it to its own ideological influence'? Lenin denies this, in face of the clearly expressed opinions of all the theorists of scientific socialism. And in that consists his enormous mistake, his theoretical fall into sin."

In order to appreciate the authority of this excommunication, you must know that Lenin himself has described Plekhanov's philosophical writings as " the best in the whole international literature of Marxism ". Nevertheless Lenin never answered Plekhanov's attack. He said four years later that it " had the obvious character of empty cavil, founded on phrases torn from their connections, and upon separate phrases not entirely happy, or not accurately formulated by me, ignoring at the same time the general content and whole spirit of the book ". But this also was no answer. The general spirit of the book is exactly what is heretical, and what makes it a turning point in the whole history of Marxism. From the first page to the last, it is the practical science of Marxism, with the metaphysics stamped under foot and ignored. Lenin's statement about the bourgeois character of the elemental movement of labour may or may not be true ; it is a statement that could not be proven. But a person thinking according to the metaphysical system of Karl Marx could not possibly conceive it as true. No matter what the passing situation may be, a dialectic materialist is bound to conceive the revolution as automatically produced by the contradictions in capitalism, and the Marxian scientist as " bringing consciousness " to the process, or " serving as its theoretical expression ". At the most he may permit this Marxian scientist to accidentally-accelerate the movement. There is not a word in Lenin's book which is even a concession to this metaphysical ideology. The book tells you " what to do ", if you want to produce with the material at hand a socialist revolution. It is a text book of practical engineering on the basis of the Marxian mechanics of history. Lenin was indeed " organically incapable of dialectic thinking ", in so far as dialectic thinking means attributing your own purposes to the external world. He was incapable of animistic thinking. He was incapable of distorting facts to fit a metaphysics. He was a practical thinker to the depth of his mind, a scientist and not a priest, an engineer and not a " midwife " of revolution.

CHAPTER V

LENIN AS AN ENGINEER OF REVOLUTION

You will notice in all the eulogies of Lenin written by Marxists, a contrast between their extravagant praise of his genius, and the small creative contribution to Marxism with which they credit him. They feel a thing which, within the limits of the economic metaphysics, they cannot define. Only after recognizing that Lenin abandoned that metaphysics, is it possible to appraise his genius, or define the details of his achievement. For this fundamental thing reappears in every one of the great innovations which he introduced into the theory and practice of Marxism.

Lenin had no sooner formed his party round a nucleus of " professional revolutionists "—defined and selected according to the purposive ideas in their minds—than he proceeded to split it upon the question whether people of a certain type should be allowed to consider themselves members. And these people again were not defined according to their economic class. They were defined according to their attitude to these purposive ideas. They were the people who talk revolution, and like to think about it, but do not " mean business ". They were the " soft " as opposed to the " hard ", the " reasoners " as opposed to the " fighters ", the " talkers " as opposed to the " workers ". Lenin proposed to eliminate them by demanding that every party member should work under the orders of the conspirative organization, accepting the full risk and discipline involved. Martov proposed a " more elastic " definition of a party member. Upon this issue the party split into " Bolsheviks " and " Mensheviks ". Martov and his followers turned out to be themselves people of just the type Lenin wanted to exclude—people who talked revolution but did not intend to produce it. And therefore the very meaning of these words " Bolshevik " and " Menshevik ", is to be found in that sharp psychological distinction made by Lenin at the beginning of his career.

" Better that ten workers should not call themselves members of the party (real workers are not so eager for position) than that one talker should have the right and the opportunity to be a party member. There is the principle which seems to me irrefutable, and which compels me to fight against Martov."

Lenin subsequently fought these Mensheviks upon a great variety of questions, and he attempted to define them in ways more in accord with the economic metaphysics. But the one element in their position which never changed, and which alone makes it possible to define them, is this psychological one. They were always seeking a formula which would enable them to talk revolution without incurring the danger of realizing it.

Thus Lenin's first innovation was to recognize the indispensable function of the man of ideas, his second innovation was to divide men of ideas into two camps, and expel without mercy those in whom ideas do not mean action. It is plain, then, that Lenin did not regard revolutionary ideas as a mere reflection of the evolution of the forces of production. A talker is just as good a reflecting apparatus as a worker. Indeed, the very use of the word " work " in order to make this all-important distinction, is a denial of the philosophy according to which revolution is an automatic product of nature's development. For work, according to the definition of Marx himself, is " a process between man and nature, in which man through his own act adjusts, regulates and controls his material intercourse with nature. He opposes himself to nature as one of her own forces. . . ." A Bolshevik, then, according to the distinction originally made by Lenin himself, is a man of Marxian ideas who opposes himself to nature with a view to regulation and control. And is there any better definition of a Menshevik than a man of Marxian ideas who is willing to let nature regulate and control him, so long as he is allowed to express and cherish these ideas ?

In forming his revolutionary party, Lenin identified and excluded another type of revolutionist whose attitude he described as the " Infantile Disease of Leftism ". This distinction was also fundamentally a psychological one, as the name implies. But, unlike the distinction between Menshevik and Bolshevik, it was originally formulated by Lenin in terms of economic class, and only received this more concrete definition in later years. At the time when Lenin formed his party, practically all the " Infantile Leftists " in Russia were opposed ·to Marxism itself. They found their natural place in the terrorist wing of the Narodniki, and the Narodniki denied, along with the entire Marxian system, the importance of the industrial proletariat. They believed in " the people " ; and the people, numerically speaking, were quite obviously the small peasant proprietors. For this reason it was possible at that time to identify and define the " infantile leftist " in orthodox Marxian fashion as a " petit bourgeois revolutionist ".

Later on, when this same psychological phenomenon appeared in Lenin's own proletarian party, the economic designation gave place more and more to the psychological. The name " revolutionists of the phrase " became a very important one with Lenin. And in 1908 a whole group was expelled from his party for the merely tactical crime of refusing to sit in a bourgeois parliament. They were described at that time as " Leftists ". And in 1920, when as a result of the successful revolution in Russia this same phenomenon made its appearance throughout the whole Bolshevik International, and became a serious menace to the tactics of the proletarian struggle, Lenin wrote his famous pamphlet defining it as " The Infantile Disease of Leftism ", and denouncing it almost exclusively in psychological terms.

I say " almost exclusively ", because Lenin began his pamphlet with a recollection of the origin of the distinction in Russia, and an orthodox Marxian definition of it.

" It is not sufficiently known abroad," he wrote, " that Bolshevism grew up, formed and hardened itself in long years of struggle against *petit bourgeois revolutionism*, which resembles or borrows something from anarchism. . . . For Marxians it is well established theoretically . . . that the small owner . . . who under capitalism is constantly oppressed and suffering, and whose conditions of life often take a sharp and rapid turn for the worse, moves easily when faced with ruin to extreme revolutionism, but is incapable of displaying consistency, organization, discipline and firmness. The petit bourgeois ' gone mad ' from the horrors of capitalism is a social phenomenon which, like anarchism, is characteristic of all capitalist countries. The weakness of such revolutionism, its futility, its liability suddenly to transform itself into obedience, apathy, phantasy, and even into a ' mad ' infatuation with some bourgeois ' fashionable ' tendency—all this is a matter of common knowledge."

Thus Lenin states at the beginning of his pamphlet the orthodox Marxian philosophy of " Leftism ". Then he departs from that philosophy, which he describes as " an abstract theoretical recognition of the truth ", into the concrete psychological investigation and definition of what Leftism in a proletarian party really is, and he never comes back to the orthodox position at all. From that point on to the last word in the last sentence— " childishness "—his pamphlet is a demonstration, not that Leftism is petit bourgeois, but that Leftism is *infantile*.

He shows these Leftists that, while they may be emotionally sincere, they are intellectually immature. They do not know how to think practically. He describes them at various points as " abstract ", " sectarian ", as substituting " purity of principle " for practicality. of tactics, as following a " tactic of mere negation ", of " opposition on principle ", satisfying themselves with " mere words ", with " revolutionary moods and dispositions ". He demonstrates the impracticality of their characteristic policies, *no compromise, down with leaders, abstention from bourgeois parliaments and reactionary trade unions, individual terrorism, illegality-for-its-own-sake*, and the like. In short he explains to them, not as a representative of the proletariat talking to representatives of the petit bourgeoisie, but as a teacher talking to his pupils, what practical thinking is, and how to do it. The real definition of " Infantile Leftism ", as it is implied throughout the body of Lenin's pamphlet, seems to me to be this : It is an attitude of immature revolutionary minds, who judge ideas and policies as an expression of the revolutionary motive and emotion, rather than as a means of achieving the revolution.

After Leftism has been defined in this way, the inference is obvious that it will appear *more often* and more characteristically among small owners " faced with ruin " and temporarily " driven mad " by the horrors of capitalism, than among proletarians systematically exploited by capitalism. To proletarians the very problem of everyday existence takes the form of a class struggle which is potentially revolutionary. And toward the problem of daily existence all healthy minds are practical, and they are capable of displaying " consistency, organization, discipline. . . ." I believe that anyone who reads Lenin's pamphlet without metaphysical predispositions, will concede that such a statement of the relation between Leftism and the economic classes, is more true to his mental attitude—as it is certainly more true to the facts—than the orthodox Marxian statement.

After the formation of his organization, the next distinctive feature of Lenin's policy was the manner in which he determined its relation to the working class. And the essence of his policy here, as it seems to me, was that instead of attempting to enlighten or " convert " the working class as a whole to communism, permitting communism to lose in this process a certain amount of its scientific clarity and revolutionary extremism, he stressed the necessity of staying with the working class personally no matter how far they wandered from the path of communism, and yet remaining intellectually distinct from them, and loyal at all times to the extreme programme of scientific revolution. This principle is best illustrated in Lenin's policy toward the trade unions. It seems a natural inference from the Marxian theory of socialism as an automatic result of the class struggle between labour and capital, that these organizations of labour should be or become socialistic. It seemed the natural business of Marxian agitators to " express " or " accelerate " this process. Lenin took the opposite view.

" Every socialist," he said, " ought so far as possible to co-operate with and actively work in these organizations. That is true, but it is not at all in our interest to demand that only socialists should be members of the ' trade ' unions. That would narrow the extent of our influence upon the mass. . . . The broader these organizations, the broader will be our influence, an influence manifested, not only through the elemental development of the economic struggle, but through the direct conscious action of the socialist members of the union upon their companions."

This is merely the common sense of a man who is completely free from the intellectualistic view of the relation of social ideas to the movement of labour. When Lenin says " our interest ", " our influence upon the mass ", he refers to an organization of people with a purposive idea, people who are trying to do something in company with the working class, and by means of it, and not merely bringing the working class a consciousness of what it is doing. Other Marxians had frequently adopted this attitude of Lenin ; no active person can be perfectly loyal to an animistic philosophy. But Lenin adopted it completely and continually, and carried it to its ultimate conclusion. His language seemed so different at first from that of the accredited priests of Marxism, that he was seriously attacked on the ground that " he never used the word proletariat in the nominative case ". Lenin had a more perfect feeling of identity with the proletariat than those who attacked him, but he could not pretend that the proletariat was doing what he was doing. A proletarian revolutionary party is not worthy of the name, he said, until it has " united leaders, class masses into one single uninterrupted whole ". But he never lost sight of the fact that this uniting is a conscious act to be performed by men of revolutionary ideas.

The same thing appears in Lenin's determination

, of the policy of his party toward the general mass of the population. He demanded that socialists should go among the masses of the people, and give expression to all their natural protests and discontent. He demanded that they should become " veritable tribunes of the people ", organizing an " all-popular indictment " of the existing regime. And when he was reproached with anti-Marxism, and asked wherein, then, will consist the class character of the movement, he replied : " Just in this, that we who organize this all-popular indictment, are socialists ; that the explanation of all the agitational questions raised will be given in an inflexibly socialist spirit, without any conscious or unconscious distortions of Marxism. . . ." Another emphatic assertion of the separate identity of the Marxian engineer, and the dynamic function of his ideas.

Lenin is alleged to have profoundly modified Marxism as a theory by recognizing the peasants and the oppressed colonial peoples as " allies " of the working class in its struggle. And yet this assertion always has to be accompanied by the remark that Marx also recognized the peasants and the colonial peoples as allies of the working class in its struggle. What then is the modification introduced by Lenin ? Simply this, that being profoundly indifferent to the metaphysical picture of the revolution as automatically produced by a resolution of " contradictions " involved in the development of industrial capitalism, Lenin was able to see the industrial proletariat, the peasants, and the colonial peoples, in their true *practical* proportions. Marx saw them in the proportions determined by a dialectic construction of which the peasants and the colonial peoples are not a perfectly integral part. Therefore his recognition of them as " allies " was incidental and inadequate in comparison with Lenin's. Marx was a metaphysician accommodating his metaphysics in a parenthesis to the demands of practical science ; Lenin was a practical scientist, ignoring altogether the metaphysics in which he believed. That is the essential difference between Lenin and Marx, so far as concerns the peasants and the colonial peoples.

The most striking feature of Lenin's political tactics was the " policy of sharp turns ". Lenin would adopt a programme, or a slogan, sufficiently fundamental to serve among ordinary politicians as the corner-stone of a republic, or the motto of a " Grand Old Party " through several generations, and then he would appear some morning a short while later and say : " The situation has changed, our programme has no further value, the slogan for the present period is as follows. . . ." Nothing like this had ever been seen before. It makes most of the great liberators appear a little wooden, a little out of gear with reality, in comparison with Lenin. It contributed more than anything else to make his political power seem occult and almost magical. And yet it was the opposite of magic ; it was the essence of scientific engineering introduced into the sphere of politics. I have shown that the distinction between scientific engineering and the practice of magic, whether in the matter of producing gold or in the matter of producing a true society, lies in the scientists' recognition and definition of an unchangeable or uncontrollable element in the given facts. There is, however, this great difference between an engineer of human history, applying the principles of Marxism, and a chemical or physical engineer—the engineer of history works with a material which is itself spontaneously changing, and he with it, in ways not irrelevant to his purpose. He cannot define once for all, except in the most general terms, the factual conditions limiting and prescribing his action. He cannot keep these conditions constant. He must therefore continually revert to the conditions, and continually redefine them, amending his procedure according to the new elements which are beyond his control. That is the significance of the " policy of sharp turns ". It is a proof that Lenin was in the full sense of the term a scientific engineer. The conjurer survived in him no more than the priest.

Lenin's Marxian eulogists usually point to the soviet form of government as the essential expression of his creative genius. The superficiality of this judgment becomes apparent when you know that during the months preceding the October revolution, pursuing his essential policy of sharp turns, Lenin was once on the point of abandoning altogether the slogan " All power to the soviets ! " The essential expression of Lenin's genius was the creation of an organization of purposive revolutionists capable of standing above and outside all such specific forms and formulations, using them or discarding them according to their transitory relation to a more general social purpose. Lenin left to " history " the decision whether the revolution should flow in the channel of the soviets or not. But he did not leave to history the decision whether the revolution should be led by the Bolshevik party. He did not leave to history the creation of that party, nor the maintenance of its entirely extraordinary character and policy. If he had, there would have been no Bolshevik revolution, as Trotsky in his " Lessons of October " has very effectively shown. I believe that no organization of men ever before exercised so profound an influence upon history in exactly the direction planned by it as the Russian Communist Party. It is an organization of a kind which never existed before. It combines certain essential features of a political party, a professional association, a consecrated order, an army, a scientific society—and yet is in no sense a sect. Instead of cherishing in its membership a sectarian psychology, it cherishes a certain relation to the predominant class-forces of society as Marx defined them. And this relation was determined by Lenin, and progressively readjusted by him, with a subtlety of which Marx never dreamed.

It seems obvious that this unique organization, with its scientifically determined equilibrium in the society surrounding it, and that unique " policy of sharp turns " successfully applied by it through a quarter of a century, is the essential expression of Lenin's creative genius. And yet the very members and heads of the party, pausing to write a tribute to Lenin, and enumerate his creative contributions to Marxism and to human history, relegate the party to a secondary position. They rarely mention its delicately adjusted relation to society, and almost never that peculiar policy which it applied with triumphant success. The reason for this is that the nature of the party, its position, and its policy of sharp turns, are all alike inconsistent with the philosophy of historic determinism. The whole situation, the whole history of the Russian revolution as it was actually lived by the members of the Bolshevik party, involved at every point a distinction between what was historically determined, and what might be done with history by this purposive organization. All practical scientific efforts involve this same distinction between what is determined and what is not. And for that reason, again, all philosophies of absolute determinism can do nothing but get in the way of practical science. The inability of Russian Marxists to state the reality about Lenin, and about their own lives, is but a further example of the obstructive foolishness of such philosophies.

It is not only the essential genius of Lenin which is distorted to meet the demands of Marxian metaphysics, but also the essential nature of the government which he founded. It is called a soviet government, and the soviets do indeed play a vital part in it. This part may increase, and the importance of the soviets in human history be very great. But it is mere academic formalism to pretend that " soviet rule " is the essence of the governmental institution established by Lenin in Russia. Its essence is the rule, within and through a soviet structure, of a disciplined and centralized organization of several hundred thousand people sworn to the purpose and trained in the science of communism, and so placed in society in relation to the dominant forces of class interest as Marx defined them, that their sovereignty is unshakable. The most significant administrative change in Russia since the October revolution, has been a gradual shifting of the centre where decisions are really made, from the " Soviet of People's Commissars ", the highest organ of the soviet structure, to the " Politburo ", the highest organ of the Communist party. And this change is nothing but the actual reality of the situation gradually breaking through the forms in which, out of loyalty to the Marxian philosophy, Lenin attempted to confine it. Until this actual reality is clearly conceived, and its significance acknowledged, I do not believe it will be possible to solve in a revolutionary manner the problems of the future development of the Bolshevik state.

" The dictatorship of the proletariat is a relentless struggle, bloody and bloodless, violent and peaceful, military and industrial, pedagogical and administrative, against the forces and traditions of the old society. The force of habit of millions and tens of millions is a most formidable force. Without a party of iron, tempered in struggle, without a party possessing the confidence of all that is honest in the class in question, without a party able to detect the moods of the mass and influence it, it is impossible to wage such a struggle with success. . . .

" Not one important political or organizational question is decided by any state institution in our republic without the governing instruction of the central committee of the party."

In those sentences you have the essence of the new kind of sovereignty established by Lenin in Russia. And you have the measure of his distance from the Marxian metaphysics. Marx declared the dictatorship of the proletariat to be an *inevitable* result of the material nature and economic situation of the proletariat. Lenin declared that without a party whose characteristics are defined in psychological and social terms, the dictatorship of the proletariat is *impossible*. And he was not deterred by considerations of metaphysical propriety any more than by considerations of democratic ideology, from giving into the hands of the party so defined, and so constituted, a position in the new state not unlike that occupied by the personal sovereign in the old.

Lenin's crowning heresy was to create this proletarian republic in a country in which capitalism is relatively undeveloped. Because of the monumental practicality of his methods, and the fundamental truth of the Marxian science, he succeeded in producing that change which is metaphysically supposed to result from a " ripening " of the " contradictions " in capitalism, in a society in which those contradictions are entirely unripe. The October revolution was a violation of Hegelian Marxism, and every success in the effort of

the Bolsheviks since the October revolution has been
a disproof of it.   For their effort has been, on the one
hand to make fast in Russia a political superstructure
and a way of thinking which are in advance of her economic development, and on the other hand to make her
catch up in economic development to this way of thinking
and this political superstructure.   No person who means
what he says seriously, and concretely, could possibly
declare that the political forms existing in Russia, and
the ideas propagated by the Communist party, are a
reflection of existing economic conditions.   Never did
a reflection put forth such gigantic efforts to produce
its likeness in the object reflected.

This fact was too flagrant to escape the attention of
Lenin's Marxian critics, and he therefore found himself
engaged at the end of his career, just as he had been
at the beginning, in a polemic which compelled him to
give expression to his fundamental intellectual attitude.
He found himself compelled to choose between metaphysical Marxism and the thoughts of a practical mind.
And he chose, as always, the thoughts of a practical
mind.

Accusing his critics of " slavish imitation of the past ",
he wrote :

" How utterly mechanical is that idea which they learned
by heart during the development of western European
social democracy, that we in Russia have not yet grown up
to socialism, that we lack—as various learned gentlemen
among them express it—the objective economic premises for
socialism.   And it does not come into anybody's head to ask
himself : Might not a people, encountering a revolutionary
situation such as was created during the imperialist war,
under the influence of the hopelessness of its situation, throw
itself into such a struggle as opened to it even the barest
chance of some slightly unusual conditions for the further
growth of civilization ? . . .

" If the creation of socialism demands a definite level of culture (although nobody can say just exactly what that definite level is) then why can we not begin by winning with a revolution the premises for that definite level of culture, and then afterward, on the basis of the workers and peasants' power and the soviet structure, set out to catch up to the other peoples ? "

There is not a word here to which a practical man, desiring to create a socialist civilization, could object. But for a Marxian metaphysician, taught to believe that the world process is logical, and that its moving force is a dialectic necessity of self-resolution of the contradictions inherent in the capitalist system of industry when they have reached their full development, there is not a syllable of satisfaction.

" No social formation ever disappears," says Marx, " before all the productive forces are developed for which it has room, and new higher relations of production never appear before the material conditions of their existence are matured in the womb of the old society."

" The organization of the revolutionary elements as a class presupposes the finished existence of all the productive forces which can be developed in the bosom of the old society."

" Law can never be on a higher level than the economic conditions and the degree of social civilization corresponding to it."

" The industrially more developed country reveals to the less developed the image of its own future."

That is dialectic materialism. That is history proceeding according to the logic of the metaphysician.

Why can we not " begin " by organizing the revolutionary elements as a class, says Lenin, and not only that, but winning the revolution, and establishing higher relations of production, and passing laws that are on a level above our economic state, and showing the industrially more advanced nations an image of their own future, and then " afterward set out to catch up to the other peoples " in the matter of developing the productive forces ?

That is Bolshevism. That is history as it was made in a certain concrete situation by an organization of men who took the ideas of Karl Marx as instrumental science, and not as animistic philosophy.[1]

A further quotation from the same article will reveal the precise method by which Lenin managed to " believe in " this philosophy, while completely ignoring it in his practical thoughts and actions. He managed this by making its meaning more abstract and general in proportion as, taken concretely and specifically, it got in his way.

[1] It is important to note that Trotsky does not fall far behind Lenin in his ability to ignore the Marxian philosophy of history. He says in a recent discussion (Pravda, Feb. 2, 1926): " The social form of our industry is immeasurably higher than that of the United States. There a mad capitalist exploitation and the most terrible inequality of classes ; here a form of industry such as opens the road to full equality of living conditions for the whole people. But in America in the frame of the capitalist form, there exists the highest technique. With us in the frame of the socialist or transitional form, an extremely backward technique. And the extent of that backwardness we ought to keep constantly before our eyes : not in order to drop our hands in despair, but in order to double our efforts in the struggle for technique and culture . . . The technique of America combined with the soviet social regime would give us not only socialism—it would give us communism, or at least it would bring very close those conditions of life in which each would work according to his abilities and receive according to his needs."

A more perfect contradiction of the Marxian philosophy of history, according to which social forms are " determined " by the evolving technique of industry, could hardly be imagined —nor a more sensible attitude to the actual problem.

" What if the complete hopelessness of their situation, multiplying ten-fold the strength of the workers and peasants, opened to them the possibility of a different transition to the creation of the basic premises of civilization from that of all western European nations ? . . . Would that change the general line of development of world history ? "

In other words, what if the events in Russia directly contradict the dogmas of dialectic materialism ? Can we not interpret those dogmas in a more general sense, a sense general enough, indeed, and loose enough, and inconsequential enough, so that they will include the events in Russia, and thus enable us to retain our metaphysical belief over and above our real thoughts and actions ?

This is the way in which every believer in animistic religion reconciles his belief with the concrete realities which contradict it. Cardinal Manning lays down the following dogma : " Ask in faith and perfect confidence and God will give us what we ask." And when the crude facts fall out to the contrary he says :

" God has said that He will give you whatsoever you ask ; but the form in which it will come, and the time in which He will give it, He keeps in His own power. . . . Sometimes it may be a chastisement, or a loss, or a visitation against which our hearts rise, and we seem to see that God has not only forgotten us, but has begun to deal with us in severity. Those very things are the answer to our prayers."

The purpose is different, but the mental process here is the same. Cardinal Manning generalizes the idea of an answer to prayer in order to cover all possible contingencies. Lenin generalizes the idea of history as determined by the development of the forces of production, in order to cover the Russian revolution. And there is not the slightest doubt that if Lenin happened to be able to produce a Communist revolution all over Europe and Asia and Africa and America and in the islands of the South Sea—a revolution which contradicted in no matter what fashion this Hegelian philosophy—he would push the philosophy still farther up into the sky, and perhaps end by forgetting it altogether. For he had no real interest in it. He was interested only in the freedom it gave him to use his mind instrumentally in a perpetually changing situation. He was interested in the one wisdom which Hegelism did contribute to a real science of thinking, the maxim that " truth is always concrete ". And it is just that maxim that he violates when he tries to maintain that Marxism, although not applicable to the concrete " transition " effected in Russia, remains true of the " general line of development of world history ".

To me the fundamental difference between Marx and Lenin is visible on almost every page they wrote. It is not a contradiction, but a difference of mental attitude. And it is not a complete difference, because Marx had in him the practical scientist, and Lenin never consciously got rid of the metaphysician. But it is a difference of all the more importance to Marxians. It may be summed up in the following two quotations about the dictatorship of the proletariat :

Marx says : " The new thing that I did consisted in demonstrating . . . that the class struggle inevitably leads to the dictatorship of the proletariat."

Lenin says : " Marx's teaching about the class struggle leads inevitably to a recognition . . . [that] the overthrow of the bourgeoisie is attainable only through the transformation of the proletariat into a ruling class."

Marx states that such a thing will happen in such a way. Lenin states that such is the only way to make it happen. Marx attributes his purpose to the external world, and tries to convert the facts and methods of action which make its realization possible, into a proof of its certainty. Lenin assumes that the revolutionary purpose exists in revolutionary people, and shows them those facts in the external world, and those methods of action, which make its realization possible. In Marx the Hegelian metaphysician was dominant over the practical scientific thinker ; in Lenin the scientific thinker gained the victory. And that victory is the theoretical foundation of Bolshevism. Bolshevism is an unconscious, and therefore incomplete, substitution of a practical science of revolution for that revolutionary philosophy of the universe which Marx created.

CHAPTER VI

LENIN'S PHILOSOPHY

LENIN compensated for his practical betrayals of the Marxian philosophy, by asserting it theoretically with extreme and violent dogmatism. He is far more rigid in his "belief" in Dialectic Materialism than Marx and Engels were. "How young is all human history," says Engels, "and how ridiculous it would be to wish to ascribe any absolute validity to our present views. . . ." Lenin says : "From that philosophy of Marxism, poured from a single chunk of steel, you cannot withdraw one fundamental premise or one essential piece, without departing from objective truth, and falling into the arms of the bourgeois-reactionary lie."

In this extreme spirit Lenin defended in philosophy exactly the opposite proposition from that which rests at the bottom of his politics. His politics is founded upon a belief in the dynamic function of revolutionary ideas, and of the men who make it a profession to realize them.

"Without a revolutionary theory there can be no revolutionary movement. . . . The statement that no efforts even of the most inspired ideologist can distract the workers' movement from the path determined by . . . material forces, is equivalent to a renunciation of socialism. . . . In what consists the rôle of the social-democracy, if not in being the 'spirit' . . . raising the elemental movement up to its programme ? "

That is the foundation of Lenin's politics. And here is his philosophy :

" The world is an ordered movement of matter, and our knowledge, being the highest product of nature, is able only to reflect that movement . . . Social consciousness *reflects* social existence, there is the substance of Marx's teaching."

Doubtless many volumes of Hegelian higher nonsense may be written in the effort to reconcile these statements, but in the end the statements will remain contradictory. Lenin defended in philosophy a position inconsistent with his fundamental attitude in politics. And although his attention was called to it, he never attempted to resolve this inconsistency. He instinctively ignored it, or chose to leave it standing. Why? Because for a revolutionist lacking the conception of a genetic science of the mind, that was the most practical thing to do.

Lenin defended the assertion that ideas are the mere automatic reflection of things, not because he had thought about ideas, and examined them, and decided that that is what they are. He would have been the last man to be deluded by so unreal an account of anything he had examined. He defended that assertion because he saw no alternative except to say that ideas *are* the reality, and that material things are secondary and a delusion. He regarded the question " How can mind know matter? " as a real question, which has but two answers : Either mind is the reality, and matter a kind of illusory product or predicate of it ; or matter is the reality and mind an automatic reflection of it. And he knew that of these two answers the latter is more akin to the scientific view, the view of anybody who seriously intends to change the world. The former leads directly into religion and the disposition to get into a comfortable relation with the world as it is. He chose the more hard-headed, practical, and scientific of those two answers to the question, " How can mind know matter? "

But if you adopt the scientific point of view thoroughly, and as it really exists in the minds of scientists at work, the question " How can mind know matter ? " is simply a meaningless question. It is a question that was asked for the sole purpose of giving the idealistic answer. It has the same significance for a science of psychology that the question, " How can a hen lay an egg ? " has for a science of physiology—namely, none at all. In permitting themselves to be led into the discussion of a meaningless question, the dialectic materialists deserted the scientific point of view, and they never got back to it. They never got back to the real question " How *does* a mind know matter—and *why* ? " And hence Lenin, educated as a dialectic materialist, remained unaware of the existence of a natural science which would have supported his assertion of the dynamic function of ideas.

The conception of conscious thought as an instrument of adaptation produced by material nature in the evolution of living organisms, just as other organic functions are produced, is a product and a continuation of that hard-headed confrontation of scientific facts, which Lenin tried to defend in his philosophy. And it is the very thing that he asserted in his politics. With this conception Lenin could have escaped from the inconsistency between his philosophy and his politics. He could have got rid of the Marxian metaphysics which tended to impede him as an engineer, without falling into the idealistic metaphysics which would impede him as a revolutionist. He could have got rid of all metaphysics, and become consciously and theoretically, what he was in actual fact, a revolutionary engineer.

If there is a " philosophy " involved in recognizing the origin and biological function of human intelligence, it consists in dismissing as meaningless a number of

questions which are meaningless, and learning to say
" I do not know ", in response to all those questions of
which you do not know the answer. It is a method
rather than a philosophy, a method which I have described as affirmatively sceptical, because it is sceptical
of philosophy, and of the attempts of philosophy to
prescribe forms or limits to science, but it affirms the
validity and believes in the development of science. In
my opinion this philosophy that is a method, would have
been far more grateful to Lenin's temperament, than
that surreptitiously animistic materialism in which he
felt compelled to believe. One thing is certain, and
that is that Lenin did not depend for the strength of
his purpose upon a metaphysical conviction that the
material world was co-operating with him. " The elemental workers' movement goes straight toward subjection to the bourgeoisie ", he said. " Our task is to
drag it away." Intellectually you may insist that this
was but a temporary lapse from the Marxian ideology ;
but a person emotionally dependent upon that ideology
could not possibly have committed this lapse. The idea
so much reiterated by our *literati* who have visited Lenin,
that he derived his heroic force from a metaphysical
conviction of the certainty of the future communist
state, is in my opinion pure romantic nonsense. Certainty
of success is the natural accompaniment of a gigantic
will, but metaphysics was merely a weapon in Lenin's
hand.

The most original thing about his book of philosophy,
is the startling way in which he asserts this very fact.
He asserts that all philosophy is a weapon of " party
struggle ", and Marx's philosophy no exception. " From
first to last Marx and Engels were partisan in philosophy ",
he says, and they made no pretence to the contrary, and
that is their merit. For such a thing as a " non-partisan

philosophy " does not exist. " The newest philosophy
is just as partisan as the philosophy of two thousand
years ago."

I have already discussed the semi-theological tricks
by which Hegel enabled Lenin to assert that his philosophy
is an instrument for winning a temporary struggle, and
at the same time assert that it is objectively true. In
that he was merely orthodox. And yet in the abandon
with which he asserts that the whole thing is " partisan "
—the Russian word is " party " rather than partisan, and
actually belongs to the political arena—he is to my
feeling very unlike Marx and Engels. And he is unlike
them in the manner in which he lives up to this statement. He blends together all through his book the
question whether dialectic materialism is *true*, and the
question whether it is *revolutionary*. He shows, or
attempts to, that it is the unconscious assumption of
the " immense majority of natural scientists ", and he
shows at the same time that it is an instrument delicately
and most adroitly adjusted for winning the victory of
the working class. He does these two things in the
same breath, in the same sentence, and without any
apparent sense of the difference. Marx and Engels
envisaged these two questions separately. They believed
that the objective truth is revolutionary, but they inferred
this from a system of philosophy which they attempted
to establish, as other philosophies are established, on
objective grounds. I cannot imagine Marx and Engels
contrasting *objective* truth with *bourgeois-reactionary*
falsity, as Lenin does in that sentence I quoted : " You
cannot withdraw one fundamental premise . . . without
departing from objective truth and falling into the arms
of the bourgeois-reactionary lie." Marx and Engels were
too well schooled in the ways of philosophy to write a
sentence like that. The difference is doubtless one of

degree. You may say that Lenin was more enthusiastic about being partisan, and less concerned about being philosophic, than Marx and Engels were.

And that is an extremely significant difference. For if you dismiss Hegelian theological tricks altogether, and come back to your own natural intelligence, what does it mean to say that all philosophy is partisan, and your own no exception ? Does it not mean that you do not believe in philosophy ? It is obvious to anybody but a Super-Logician that in order to have an authentic existence, and be capable of definition, philosophy must be non-partisan. It must rise above the interests of either side in a temporary struggle. If Lenin never made a statement which *was* non-partisan and *did* rise above the interests of his side in the class struggle, we might perhaps accept this partisan thing called dialectic materialism as his nearest approach to philosophy. But when he says that this thing is an instrument of temporary struggle, when he says that all philosophy is partisan, he has uttered a non-partisan opinion. That opinion is his real philosophy. And it is not a philosophy of dialectic materialism. It is a philosophy of affirmative scepticism—an intellectual attitude which denies the validity of philosophy, while affirming the validity of the science which understands it. It is exactly the attitude which is forced upon a man who knows the biological origin and function of his own intelligence, the attitude of a scientist who includes genetic psychology in his equipment. That is why I think this attitude would have been more grateful to Lenin's mind than the animistic metaphysics which he felt compelled to assert, and which he asserted with excessive and unnatural dogmatism.

CHAPTER VII

ADVANTAGES OF A SCIENTIFIC ATTITUDE

THE conscious substitution of a Marxian science of revolution for the Hegelian philosophy of Marx, will increase some of the difficulties of the revolutionary movement. It will increase for the intelligentsia the difficulty of organizing their emotions to meet the demands of a class struggle. The motives which bring various people of ideas into the revolutionary struggle are widely different, and yet in order to function there with force and permanence, they must all acquire a feeling of their identity with the struggling class. A philosophy which represents the entire recorded history of humanity as consisting of this struggle, and the universe itself as concerned in its resolution through the dictatorship of the proletariat, is no doubt a help in this process. It is significant, however, that Lenin who was so careless of that philosophy, identified himself with the struggling masses more directly, and with less blab and protestation, than many of the more Hegelian Marxists. It is possible that a study of the real psychological problems involved, would be as helpful in the end as this ideological self-deception.

Another loss will be that religious certainty of success, which Hegelian Marxism gives to some of the soldiers of the revolution. " Trust God and keep your powder dry ", is the slogan with which soldiers have always been led into battle. " Trust Economic Determinism and keep your powder dry ", fits the same way into the mind. _ " Keep your powder *dry* ", is more heroic. It is easy to exaggerate the emotional importance of mental attitudes, however. When Rosa Luxemburg said that the workers' movement derives its strength and courage " above all " from a conviction of the objective necessity of the social revolution, she undoubtedly expressed a genuine emotion. And the emotion is not uncommon among philosophic Marxians. But that does not prove that her statement is true. Nothing could be more improbable than that the workers' movement, or she herself, or any other great revolutionist, derives his strength and courage essentially from a philosophic conviction.

Whatever may be lost in getting rid of the relics of animism, will be more than compensated by the advantages of a consciously practical and scientific attitude. Aside from the general advantage of basing oneself upon fact, and living in the real world, unloading a mountain of cant and conscientious sophistry, and becoming clear-minded and capable of unlimited growth, there are certain specific revolutionary advantages in abandoning metaphysical habits of thought. It is, for one thing, the only way to achieve that " maximum of flexibility " toward which Lenin aspired. Anyone who feels compelled to reconcile his practical efforts to change the world, with a theoretical conception of the world as changing itself, can never achieve that maximum, no matter how bold or how skilful he may be at slipping out of the clutches of his own theory. All the thinking of the Third International since the Russian revolution has been confined within the limits of the formula : " This is the period of the break-down of capitalism." That formula belongs to the metaphysics of Marxism. It imputes to history a systematic procedure towards communism of which there is no scientific evidence, and it imputes to the leaders of the Third International a knowledge in advance of this procedure, which they could not possibly possess. A completely practical mind would have no disposition to confine itself in such a formula. It might, if the evidence were convincing, declare that " capitalism is breaking down ". But in the circumstances that actually existed at the time when this formula was adopted, the simple and scientific statement would have been : " We can break capitalism down now." That was the actual attitude of Lenin's mind, and of his nerves and muscles, when he adopted the intellectual formula : " This is the period of the breakdown of capitalism."

The example is timely, because just at the present moment it is apparently not possible to break capitalism down. And all the brains of the Third International must be employed in deciding the inconsequential question, whether to revise the original formula " This is the period of the break-down of capitalism ", or to adhere to the formula, but extend the duration of the conceived " period ". History knows nothing about periods, and the simple fact is that the Third International is waiting and preparing for another chance to do what it wants to do. Until that fact is theoretically conceived, as well as practically acted upon, the " maximum of flexibility " will not be achieved.

Another advantage in getting rid of the relics of animism, is that it will relieve Marxists of a fear of the developments of science. It will enable them to meet the attacks of scientists on their own ground. It is not impossible that the achievements of psychology in this century, basing itself upon the physiology of the nervous system, will compare in their interest with those of the physical sciences in the nineteenth. It is certain that they will attract increasing attention. Being genetic in its fundamental character, this science will have nothing but ridicule for Hegel's antiquated theory of the mind. Marxists will thus find themselves, not " in the forefront of the science of their day ", as they have always boasted of being, but in the backwash clinging to an abandoned piece of intellectual baggage. An exchange of arguments between the Bolshevik editor, Bukharin, and the Russian physiologist, Pavlov, illustrated this weakness of the Marxian position. Bukharin, conceding that Pavlov is scientific in his own field, accused him of approaching sociology, not scientifically, but with a bourgeois class-prejudice. As Bukharin's own sociology is nothing but a metaphysical apotheosis of proletarian class-prejudice, the argument carried no conviction whatever. It had no clarity, and it had no weight. If Marxism were a science, Bukharin could answer Pavlov in the manner he attempted to, and with overwhelming force. For Pavlov himself desires a drastic reconstruction of social relations, and looks to science to lay the foundation for it.

" Only the final science," he says in one of his books, " the exact science of man himself . . . will lead him out of the present darkness, and purify him of the present disgrace in the sphere of human relations."

To this the reply is obvious : It is exactly that science of man himself—the very biological foundation of it— which proves the necessity of a proletarian dictatorship as the first step out of the present darkness. In your laboratory you know that man is first of all an animal engaged in the struggle for life. Know this same fact outside your laboratory, and your efforts to escape from " the present disgrace in the sphere of human relations " must inevitably take the course outlined by Marx.

It is not only psychology that Marxians fear, but they fear any perfectly objective investigation into the nature of anything whatever. Having projected their purpose into a description of things in general, they are compelled, in order to defend that purpose, to defend this description. In a preface to his " Anti-Dühring ", Engels recounts his enormous labour of seven year defending this description — translating all modern science, that is, into the terms of the Marxian dialectic. He concludes somewhat pathetically that the task has become too great for one man. In Soviet Russia a whole coterie of men, constituting almost a professional revolutionary-philosophic priesthood, are devoting themselves to it. A continual stream of abstruse volumes and a monthly magazine of the highest philosophic technicality bear witness to their labours. It would be difficult to imagine a more futile employment of the human mind than this " going over " of the whole body of organized knowledge, restating every finding that cannot be doubted or otherwise disposed of, in the form of an analogy to the proletarian revolution. For that is what this process amounts to, once you have dispensed with Hegel's original and rather more practical purpose of " rising to God out of the empirical view of the world ". Instead of issuing the command to contemporary science, " Give all you've got in the name of the working class ! " the Russian Communists issue the command, " Give nothing but the Negation of the Negation or we fire ! "

All this incredible professorial hocus-pocus, associated so incongruously with the enterprise of revolution, is the result of fear. The fear was expressed by Lenin himself in an article which he wrote for that monthly magazine of philosophy when it was founded. Its task should be, he said, to find the answers to " those philosophic questions which are created by the transformation of natural science, and by way of which the intelligentsia, prone to worship bourgeois fashions, slips into the reaction ". For this purpose he advised the editors to " organize a systematic study of the dialectic of Hegel from the materialist point of view ". Is it not surprising, that, in order to defend his revolution against modern bourgeois fashions, arising out of the latest developments of science, Lenin should call in the help of a bourgeois professor whose reactionary disquisitions, based on the developments of science, were fashionable a hundred years ago ? Lenin's opinion of bourgeois professors in general is this : " Not one of them . . . *is to be trusted to the extent of one word*, once the question of philosophy arises. . . . Professors of philosophy are the learned errand-boys of the theologians." And yet because he cannot simply posit the existence of his own revolutionary purpose, Lenin has to fall back on one of the most obedient of these errand-boys of theology to defend the science of revolution. Lenin's revolutionary will had no need of help from Hegel. It had no reason to fear science, nor the philosophic questions arising out of an attempt to generalize science. Once that revolutionary will is understood to reside in revolutionists, and not in the universe, the free and unlimited efforts of scientists to understand the universe can only be a help to it. These real efforts, moreover, can be distinguished directly, and without the aid of any study of the Hegelian dialectic, from the attempts of metaphysical professors to implant animistic purposes in the universe. Instead of fighting one form of animism with another, you can fight animism with science, and all the metaphysical professors—Hegel and the soviet priesthood with the rest—can be dismissed as a superfluity and a nuisance. In their place a corps of real teachers can dedicate themselves to the immortal revolutionary ideal of Bakunin— that science should become " one in fact with the immediate and real life of all individuals ".

CHAPTER VIII

THE ATTITUDE TO RELIGION, ART AND MORAL IDEALS

AN abandonment of materialistic animism will enable the revolutionary science to defend itself in a true way against religious belief. The present way is to root out all warm and personal religions, and at the same time destroy wonder and a sense of the world's mystery, by putting a cold and impersonal religion in their place. No human being not specifically and professionally occupied with the revolutionary struggle will accept such a religion as this of dialectic materialism. It has therefore no value whatever as an antidote to the " opium of the people ". But a great many human beings—we do not know how many—will accept instruction in the distinction between animism and science, and will agree to adopt the scientific view-point, if you can show them what it really is. You leave them their freedom of feeling—which they will retain in any case— but you convince them that science and practical wit are the only forms of knowledge, and that the only way to get anything done is to do it.

Abandoning the Marxian philosophy will also put the revolution in a true attitude towards art and poetry. The present attitude is to declare that, since the essential general reality of life and history is the economic class struggle, there can be no real art or poetry which is irrelevant to it.

" In the great struggle of classes which is developing throughout the entire world," says a recent manifesto from Moscow, " there are and there can be no neutrals. Art, which has always served and still serves as a powerful instrument for educating the sentiments of the masses, in harmony with the problems and the situation of this or that class, can not escape from participation in this great battle of world history." Upon this basis the literary artists of all countries are summoned to organize an " International of Proletarian World Literature ".

In other words art and poetry, having with difficulty escaped from their bondage to religion, must now enter into bondage to politics. They must be regarded as subordinate to a single practical enterprise. No great or consecrated poet or artist in the world could sincerely subscribe to such a manifesto. Poetry and art may contribute vitally to purposive effort, but they are in their essence and definition distinct from it and independent of it. Their interest is in experience and not purpose, in being and not becoming. The only ultimate distinction which can be made between poetic and practical language, is that poetic language pauses to realize the existing nature of the things mentioned, practical language merely indicates them for purposes of action or adjustment. Even when a poet lends his art to an effort to change reality, the thing which he lends is a genius for enjoying, and making others enjoy, the qualities of reality as it is. That these qualities are of infinite variety, is the very basis of the possibility of his art. To tell a sensuous poet that there is but one " reality " in matter—that expressed in the words " hydrogen nuclei and electrons "—is to deny the emotional validity of his poems. And yet this formula is, after all, science and not metaphysics. To tell a poet of humanity that there is but one reality in contemporary social life and history, the class struggle, is simply ridiculous. Whatever the poet may try to do with his opinions, his art by its very nature opposes and refutes all such formulæ.

To recognize the depth and ultimateness of the distinction between poetry and science, between realization and adjustment, is in my opinion the way in which scientifically educated people can best retain their sanity. It is the way in which, unconsciously, they do retain it. Science has gradually built up a conception of the real world which deprives it of every quality that is humanly interesting. At the hands of Einstein and the higher chemistry, the " primary qualities ",—shape, motion, impenetrability—are following the " secondary qualities "—colour and sound and taste and fragrance—into the realm of the " unreal ". The " reality ", with these savants, is becoming little more than a set of mathematical formulæ. By this route, science and the attempt to generalize science, are arriving at a conception of the universe just as " idealistic " as that of the philosophers, but without the personal qualities which make the philosopher's idealistic universe interesting. No complete and living man, who wishes to imagine what he knows, will be content to live in such a universe. He will find his way out. And there are, it seems to me, but two ways out. One is to jump the gulf which divides this cold idealistic universe of science from the warmer one of metaphysics. The metaphysicians will provide abundant tackle and scaffolding for the purpose of this jump, and we shall find ourselves back again in the animistic attitude to reality. Those mathematical formulæ of Einstein will begin to speak with the tongues of angels, and their first word will undoubtedly be *Duty*. But there is another way out of that barren world offered to our imagination by science, and that is to declare the parallel and equal rights of poetry, or the pure experience of things. When science denied the "tertiary qualities"—the qualities of spirit—to the material world, it opposed itself to religion. That opposition was ultimate and essential to the nature of science, because religion like science is concerned with adjustment and tries to accomplish things. But when science denied the "secondary qualities", it opposed itself to poetry—an opposition which is not ultimate, because poetry as such is not concerned with adjustment and only seeks to realize things as they are. Far from being an enemy of science, poetry is the one thing which can sanction it, and justify the violence which it does to the obvious qualities of experience. If the moment of realization is invalid, there is not a kind of absurdity in these intellectual contortions which are only by-products of the effort to achieve it.

If this view-point is just, or can even be plausibly defended, in regard to sciences of such high generality as physics and chemistry, its validity in regard to the specific scientific enterprise of revolution, can hardly be denied. The poetry of life, and its infinite variety, far from being subordinate to this revolutionary enterprise, is the one thing which justifies it, and gives it any command upon the energies of men, no matter to what class they belong. The realizations of artists may help the revolution or oppose it, but they may also be as indifferent to it as the wind of a spring morning. All assertions to the contrary come from the theology of revolution, and not from the practical science of it. This science would indeed teach revolutionists to *use* poets and artists more often and more skilfully than they have yet been used. It would teach Marxian editors, for example, instead of demanding that every contribution to their magazines shall be coloured with the revolutionary theme, and thus confining their circulation to those specifically interested in that theme, to demand that the essential variety of life be expressed, and thus carry the revolutionary understanding among all those intellectually interested in life. " One of the greatest and most dangerous mistakes of communists," as Lenin said, " is to imagine that a revolution can be achieved by the efforts of revolutionists alone." An editor who understood the significance of these words, would rule out on principle only those contributions which have a practical meaning that is positively counter-revolutionary. To such a negative censorship the poets and artists must be asked to submit. And they will submit, whether they choose to or not, when a Marxian party is in power. In that sense they are subordinate— or to that extent their functions are postponed, just as realization is always postponed for a serious achievement. But in every other sense they are independent. And, they should defend their independence, in my opinion, both against the attempt to organize them, and against the attempt to intimidate them with a specific practical principle parading in the guise of a general theory of the universe.

A practical science of revolution would also abandon the irresponsible Marxian generalizations about morals. Real morality, as the Greeks perceived, is intelligent judgment applied to the problems of conduct, and the estimation of human character. Moral precepts will naturally vary, not only according to the maturity of the intelligence—the degree to which responsible judgment has replaced mere social custom—but also according to the conditions of each particular problem. In this science as in other practical sciences, the truth is always concrete. And no set of moral ideals, no system of ethics, can relieve each society, each class, each individual, of the task of solving specific problems.

Marxism has wisely emphasized this fact ; it has done its share to liberate mankind from absolute moral precepts. But it has very unwisely blurred the distinction between moral intelligence and mere customary judgment, and attempted to reduce the whole wisdom of personal life, along with all the other achievements of the human brain, to a mere reflection of social relations that are determined by the state of the productive forces. In the Marxian religion, all moral ideals change completely with a revolution in these forces and relations, the good becoming evil and the evil good. Indeed, according to the strictest Hegelian kind of Marxism, evil and good are but two aspects of a single dialectic process, the evil being the progressive and disturbing side—the natural dress and appellation of the revolution.

In my opinion religions in general cherish moral irresponsibility far more than they correct it. And this religion of Marxism is no exception to the rule. A revolutionist—and particularly a revolutionary leader —who believes that he is the mere expression of a change that is being taken care of by the " Productive Forces ", is far less likely to be reliable than one who understands that he is guiding a revolutionary struggle in the direction of a new society. A more explicit reliance upon professional revolutionists, is one of the changes adopted by Lenin in unconsciously abandoning the Marxian religion. Consciously abandoning this religion will increase the likelihood of their being reliable. It will make room for the instinctive sentiment and natural human opinion, that a person who undertakes to lead a class struggle toward the goal of a better society has assumed an unusual moral responsibility. Wherever the word " ought " has a meaning, it will be affirmed that such a man ought to know his own motives, and be honest with those whom he leads. Anything that weakens that intelligent sentiment and conviction, weakens the resources of the revolution. Anything that strengthens it, strengthens the revolution.

Lenin was fully aware of this. Lenin was not in the least sentimental, and therefore he was free from that over-correction of sentimentality which makes some Marxists hold themselves superior—in public discourse, at least—to the important problems of personal character. He was not afraid to say that it is necessary for a professional revolutionist to be " devoted ", " heroic ", " self-sacrificing ", " honest ".

" A demagogue," he said at the beginning of his career, " is the worst enemy of the working class . . . A man can slip into demagogism through mere political *naïveté*, and I will never stop repeating that a demagogue is the worst enemy of the working class."

And at the end of his career he said : " Without a party possessing the confidence of all that is *honest* in the class in question . . . it is impossible to wage the struggle [of proletarian dictatorship] with success."

In short, while abandoning the illusion that the success of the revolution is metaphysically inevitable, Lenin declared that without honesty in the vanguard it is actually impossible. Marxists could well blot out most of their large talk about Ethics and the Materialistic Interpretation of History, and write in its place this simple statement of fact by a practical revolutionary engineer. There is no element in the Bolshevik tactics of Lenin more vitally important than the transparent purity of his motives, and his perfect intellectual honesty before the proletariat.

CHAPTER IX

REVISIONISM AND THE FABIANS

ANOTHER enemy against which the scientific attitude would be a protection, is "revisionism". It is an attempt to amend the theories and qualify the factual judgments of Marx and Engels, in such a way as to deprive them of their revolutionary character. Edward Bernstein, the originator of this tendency, undertook to prove upon the basis of modern statistics that the fundamental contradiction in capitalism is not increasing, and that capitalism is not developing toward the inevitable crisis and conquest of power by the proletariat, which Marx predicted. At the same time he asserted that the influence of ideological, and particularly "ethical" factors in human history, is increasing, and that therefore a gradual transition to socialism, without that crisis and conquest of power, is possible. His writings were the first formidable assault upon the Marxian science and art of revolution, and they are still for people of honest and scientific intelligence, the most dangerous enemy. They have never been adequately answeied. They never can be adequately answered so long as Marxism retains its Hegelian-metaphysical character. For Bernstein speaks in the name of science, and it is impossible to prove scientifically that capitalism is evolving toward an inevitable crisis and conquest of power by the proletariat. That proposition rests upon a metaphysical foundation. On the other hand, it is impossible to *disprove* scientifically Bernstein's affirmative proposition—that an ethical evolution toward communism is possible—without having recourse to psychological knowledge. It is the genetic and real science of human behaviour which disproves the possibility of an " ethical " transition to socialism, and which alone can disprove it for a scientific mind. And since the Marxian philosophy denies the validity of this science in general, and its relevance to the understanding of history in particular, orthodox Marxists are deprived of their one real weapon against this soft-headed school.

It is the greatest misfortune in the history of Marxian theory that Bernstein combined his drift toward reformism, with an attack on the Hegelian Marxian philosophy. That philosophy was already dying a natural death among all sorts of Marxists, revolutionary and reformist alike ; but Bernstein's overt attack upon it in the name of reformism automatically revived it in the minds of all genuine revolutionists. And consequently this vast load of professorial nonsense has been zealously preserved by exactly those who had no use for it. I believe that the unnatural dogmatism of Lenin's philosophy is a direct result of Bernstein's book. If it had been a revolutionist who first opened the attack on dialectic materialism, Lenin would have been in the forefront of the movement to make Marxism scientific, and the whole intellectual apparatus and outcome of the Russian revolution would have been a generation ahead of where it is. Bernstein abandoned animism—essentially, although with a confused understanding of what he was doing—and picked up the more dangerous weapon of instrumental thinking. His opponents, instead of seizing the same weapon and understanding it better, only tightened their grip on the old arquebus, and fell back more rigorously upon the old methods of fighting. " Revisionism " therefore remains unvanquished, and flourishes as a more " scientific " kind of Marxism, although the whole history of the epoch since Bernstein's apostacy has proven that his practical proposal is absurd.

The shadow of Bernstein will never cease to haunt the minds of Marxists, until they meet him with weapons better than his own. To his pseudo-scientific slogan, " Back to Kant ! " they should answer with a scientific slogan, " Forward with the real science of the mind ! " To his assertion that the development of capitalism does not prove a proletarian dictatorship inevitable, they should reply, pointing to Russia : We need only to know that it is possible. To his assertion that the influence of the " ethical factor " is increasing and that a gradual transition by way of persuasion into socialism is possible, they should reply, pointing to the world war : We base our method upon the real nature of man.

In this way they will not only confute the revisionists, but they will recover their own honesty of mind. A Marxian with revolutionary determination will not abandon the method of class struggle toward the dictatorship of the proletariat, because it is proven to him that the number of wealthy capitalists is slightly increasing, and the number of moderate incomes also. He will not abandon this method because the petty bourgeois class is not disappearing, agriculture shows no definite tendency to centralization, and the " increasing misery " of the working class is proven to be a myth. He will not abandon his assumption that the essential feature in modern society is the class struggle, no matter how many facts of a contrary nature may be piled up in front of him, *unless and until these facts convince him that by acting upon that assumption he cannot arrive at his goal.* Nothing has been contributed by the revisionists to convince him of this. And if Marxians understood that their own theory is a plan of action, they would only welcome those important tabulations of fact which have been contributed. These tabulations are just the thing needed to make revolutionary strategy expert. But since Marxians imagine their plan of action to be an objective description of what is happening, they are compelled to deny these very facts which it is most important for them to know. Marxian generalship suffers enormously from the circumstance that its intelligence service spends more time defending a thesis, than ascertaining the facts. And since the thesis it defends is not scientifically defensible, an element of unconscious casuistry is introduced into the thoughts of the most single-minded soldiers of the revolution. A man who projects his purpose into the objective facts is always compelled, sooner or later, either to abandon his purpose or distort the facts. He has the choice between weakness of will and dishonesty of mind. Abandoning the animism of Marx, will relieve revolutionists of this unpleasant and ultimately unbearable choice.

" Fabian Socialism " is the Anglo-Saxon equivalent of revisionism. Instead of revising the revolutionary teaching of Karl Marx, the Fabians ignore it, or dismiss it with a few superior words in the name of British common sense. It has always been something of a problem for Marxists why the British intellectuals are able to carry off this attitude—why the doctrines of Marx, which in his own opinion applied most perfectly to England, have never found a substantial foothold there. They have never found a substantial foothold in America either, except among immigrants from continental Europe, and yet America is replacing England as a model of the economic development analysed by Karl Marx.

The principal reason for this, in my opinion, is the German metaphysical form of those doctrines, which does in actual fact offend our " common sense ". The whole general spirit of Anglo-Saxon intellectual culture and philosophy—notwithstanding the little bomb exploded in behalf of the Deity by Bishop Berkeley—has been matter-of-fact and scientific. This seems to be because the Anglo-Saxons are so well at ease with the hypocrisies of religion. They go to church on Sunday, or send a little money there, and having thus taken care of their soul and their property interests, they feel free to stay at home and occupy themselves with real intellectual problems. The Germans are more honest and sentimental. They feel obliged to mix God and the saints all up with pure reason and the categories of the understanding, and the result, although morally creditable, is intellectually abhorrent to an Anglo-Saxon. Hegel as a " scientific " cult never really crossed the British Channel. And Marx's philosophy, which may be described as a partial recovery from Hegel, fails to catch our interest. We never had the disease, and we cannot take an enthusiastic part in the convalescence.

In short, the idea of including our own purpose and its realization in our objective definition of the facts, is entirely alien to our minds. We simply do not know how to do it. We have the choice therefore of rejecting Marxism wholesale, or effecting a compromise between Marxism and our natural common sense, in which the real nature of Marxism is obscured, and our common sense also loses its clear outlines. Bernard Shaw adopted the former alternative. He rejected Marxism wholesale—not because he is a soft-headed socialist by temperament or natural conviction, but because he is a man of hard common sense. " A good man fallen among Fabians," Lenin called him. Most Anglo-Saxon revolutionists, including the theorists of the present British Communist party, have adopted the other alternative. They have tried to become Marxists and at the same time remain sensible and scientific-minded Britons. The result is that a veil has been drawn over the philosophic aspects of Marx's position, and very few people in the English-speaking world know or believe that Marxism really is what it is—a rationalistic philosophy of the universe. If Marxism became a concrete practical science, this dilemma would be removed. Both the scorn and the ignorance of Marxism among English-speaking intellectuals would begin to disappear, and Anglo-Saxon common sense might make a significant contribution to the development of a science of revolution.

CHAPTER X

MENSHEVIKS

A MORE subtle enemy of revolutionary science than its open rejection, or the attempt to destroy it by " revision ", is the Menshevik betrayal of it. I have already shown that the distinction between Menshevik and Bolshevik can only be defined psychologically, and that Lenin originally so defined it. It seems to me of great importance, not only to revolutionary science, but to human wisdom in general, that this distinction should be really understood. It does not belong merely to politics, but can be made wherever human beings gather together on the basis of belief in a radical or extreme idea.

The belief in ideas has two contrary functions in our emotional life, and those in whom it fulfills one function will inevitably part at the moment of action from those in whom it fulfills the other. We erect an idea in our minds because we are ill-at-ease or at pain in the circumstances of reality. The original function of the idea was to guide us in an effort to change the reality fundamentally and so get relief. But in order to fulfill this function, the idea itself must have for us a certain reality. We must be able to love it, linger upon it, adhere to it in social groups, sacrifice our time and money, and even our respectability, to its cultivation. And in this process we often manage to alleviate the pain of the reality without fundamentally changing the reality itself. We do this with the greater ease if we are " intellectual ", and ideas are very real to us. They become a kind of daily companion and redeemer of our world, consoling us with an extreme " belief " about its future, and yet leaving us free to patch it up in little ways less difficult and more ready to our hand.

It is obvious that while employing an idea in this latter fashion, we shall resent any attempt to rob that idea of its purity which is essentially its ideality. We shall resent with equal violence the attempt to prove that the idea is incapable of realization, and the attempt actually to realize it—because either of these attempts, if successful, will destroy its value as an object of devout attention, a love and consolation in the pain and ugliness of what is real.

Plato was an intellectual of this static type. But he was conscious of the fact, and boldly declared that ideas were more interesting and more real to him than things. He had no method, and he had no need of a method, for realizing his Ideal Republic. The modern Menshevik is not conscious of his character. He has not the bold mysticism of Plato, and he has a method for realizing his ideal. The method as well as the ideal enters into the substance of his belief. It is a belief about a real future. And when that method begins to be actually applied, when that future begins to show its harsh substance in the present, this unconscious Platonist finds himself in a very embarrassing position. He has solved his problem of life by *believing in* an idea. He has perhaps made it his profession to believe in it. And he is compelled in defence of his vital equilibrium, in defence of his very personality—for the belief is deep and sincere—to resist those who undertake to change that idea into a fact. He is compelled to play the

part of a hypocrite.   But he is not a hypocrite ; he is
something far more complex and obstructive than that.
He is a Menshevik.

If Marxians will accept this much psychology as a
fact, they will soon see that in the struggle against Menshevism, as well as in the struggle against revisionism,
they are hampered by their philosophy.   That philosophy
involves their keeping up two kinds of knowledge at the
same time.   One is the concrete knowledge of facts and
probabilities, discovered, organized, and defined with a
view to guiding their own purposive action.   The
other is an abstract knowledge of the world process,
supposed to include that purposive knowledge and also
the action based on it, and assure them of the certainty
of its success.   Marxists dart back and forth between
these two kinds of knowledge, and the art of dodging
so rapidly as never to get cornered in either one, is what
it means to be a highly trained and irrefutable Marxian.
. . . But this simultaneous cultivation of two kinds of
knowledge gives the Menshevik exactly the opportunity
that he wants.   He wants to believe in Marxism, and
agitate and work for it, up to the point where he comes
in danger of producing a result, and then find a way
out.   A very simple way out is to abandon the purposive science altogether, and take refuge in the animistic
philosophy.   That is what Mensheviks have done
almost without exception in the revolutionary period
just past.

" In view of the situation created by the war," said
Lenin, " we can produce the revolution we have been
working for in Russia now ! "

" The world process is not yet producing the revolution in Russia ! " was the answer of the Mensheviks.
" Capitalism is not yet ripe ! "

Nothing could be more simple.   Nothing could be

more obvious than the service which this animistic philosophy extends to those who wish to believe in the revolution, without incurring the danger of realizing it. At any moment they can throw off upon the " historical process " their own responsibility for action.

" There is to-day," says Kautsky, attacking the Bolsheviks, " only one revolutionary theory of society, that of Karl Marx. . . . Now what this theory teaches us is that our desires and capabilities are limited by material conditions, and it shows how powerless is the strongest will which would rise superior to them."

Says Lenin : " Kautsky, in the guise of an ' economic analysis ', with proud words about ' historical materialism ', is now advocating the subjection of the workers to the bourgeoisie."

This merely reproduces the old conflict with Plekhanov. And that, you remember, was but a continuation of the life-long struggle of Marx's own mind against his metaphysical training. Every time that a real man of action makes use of the Marxian science, he is compelled by some trick or other to get rid of that animistic survival. Marx himself cried, " I am not a Marxist ! " Wilhelm Liebknecht pleaded his own lack of education—he had been too busy to study Hegel ! Lenin accused the philosophic Marxists of " cavilling ", of " pedantry ", of " slavish imitation of the past ", and carried the day by violent assertion. Trotsky accuses them of " fatalistic optimism ", of " formless determinism "—whatever that may be. He calls them " bad revolutionists ", because they " expect the revolutionary character of the epoch to help them ". And in Russia he imputes to them a " scholastic parody " of Marxism which " consists in converting a conditional and limited thought of Marx—that ' advanced nations reveal to

backward nations the image of their own future '—
into a kind of absolute super-historical law . . . and
upon that law trying to found the tactics of the party
of the working class ". This particular thought of
Marx occurs in a profoundly thoughtful preface to the
first edition of " Das Kapital ". It occurs in the sentence immediately following that in which he speaks
of the immanent laws of capitalist production, which
" carry themselves through with iron necessity ". It
belongs quite obviously to the very essence of the
metaphysics of the revolution as a necessary result
of the ripening of contradictions in capitalism. To
call this a " limited and conditional thought of Marx "
is merely a way of saying that you do not take that metaphysics seriously.

Karl Radek has another way of saying the same thing :

" When can the social revolution begin ? " he asks. " It
can begin and it does begin in every country where the
conditions created by capitalism for the workers are unen-
durable. The sufferings of the people make little account
of the statistics of Cunow & Co ; the revolutionary volcano
does not delay its eruptions until the Marxists and doctors
of statistics give the signal. The man who with tables of
statistics goes about to prove the impossibility of a social
revolution only proves how very imperfectly he has understood his Marx."

Obviously a simpler way to say all these things is this :
The philosophy of dialectic materialism is not to be
confused with the practical science of Marxism, and
wherever and whenever it gets in the way, it is to be
kicked out. By becoming theoretically conscious of
their actual mental attitude, the Bolsheviks could get
this philosophy out of their way permanently and without
casuistry. Instead of dodging around the theoretical

stronghold of Menshevism with a series of unconvincing intellectual tricks, they would simply abandon that stronghold to the Mensheviks, and to the past—where it naturally belongs—and go forward as the sole exponents of scientific Marxism.

CHAPTER XI

BUREAUCRATISM AND REVOLUTIONARY EDUCATION

AFTER the conquest of power, a new danger to revolutionary progress arises in the form of bureaucratism in the proletarian government. And this danger is greater in proportion to the sovereign part played by a party of revolutionists within that government. So long as that party " unites leaders with class with masses in one single uninterrupted whole "—to quote again the phrase of Lenin—its dictatorship is in reality a dictatorship of the proletariat. But this union, which was comparatively easy to achieve in the days of struggle, becomes difficult to preserve after the victory. The leaders of the party are now suddenly transformed from disreputable rebels to sovereign officials and captains of industry. A tendency to confirm and solidify their own power, not only at the expense of the proletariat as a whole, but even of the rank and file membership of the party, is inevitable. It is probably by this road that working-class revolutions—and especially those conducted according to the organizational principles of Lenin—will most often tend to relapse. Instead of going forward with the creation of a new proletarian-democratic society, they will tend to establish the dictatorship of a group, in whose minds the ideas of Marx—dynamic in the past—will degenerate into ideological phrases. A pious repetition of these ideological phrases will tend to replace the active science of revolution, and provide a cover for the rebirth of the old system. This new difficulty—which is really a kind of post-revolutionary Menshevism—ought not to discourage people in their scientific efforts, but it ought to be recognized and prepared against by all vigilant revolutionists. Bureaucratism, with its accompaniment of ideological revolutionary piety, ought to take its place with Menshevism, Revisionism, and the " Infantile Left ", among the standing enemies of the proletarian revolution.

That the Hegelian-Marxian metaphysics plays straight into the hands of this enemy, needs no demonstration. Being a religion, it is the natural property of a priestly caste. Its pretence that science is something else besides a perfection of the natural process of thinking—that wisdom is, in fact, a mysterious art discovered in Germany by a professorial wizard entirely unintelligible to simple men—automatically divides the revolutionary culture into two parts. There is the esoteric doctrine, property of the few who have learned to " think dialectically ", and there is the vulgar gospel for the common people. Hegel himself said that his philosophy presupposed " a higher level of culture than ordinary ", and this view was substantially carried over into dialectic materialism. " The art of operating with ideas," says Engels, " is not inborn, and it is not bestowed with ordinary everyday consciousness." And his American translator adds : " So removed is the point of view of the writer of these pages from that of the man in the street that it is doubtful whether it is possible for more than a comparatively few students thoroughly to grasp the significance of the dialectic and apply it in a satisfactory and effective fashion." Kautsky preached a distinction between Marxism as " cheaply and vulgarly understood ", and the Marxism of those who have acquired sufficient knowledge and striven faithfully enough, to " resolve the contradiction between the surface and the essence of things ". Plekhanov expressly divided the Marxian theory " as it may be stated in popular speech " from the true doctrine. And even Lenin, who had as little natural taste for the esoteric as anyone who ever lived, was compelled to concede that an inferior discipline called formal logic " must continue to be taught, with amendments, to the lower grades in the schools ".

All this mystification militates directly against the formation of a proletarian-democratic society. It not only withdraws from the masses the right to understand their own revolution, but it withdraws from them the right to all scientific understanding. I have already described the work of the soviet philosophers in their technical books and journals of dialectic materialism. It is a work of obscurantism. The simple-hearted reader who would like to cherish the hope of understanding a little science some day, may imagine the nebulous empyrean into which that hope recedes when the theories of Einstein have been translated into the terms of the Hegelian dialectic. As a result of the greatest popular revolution in history, science is being darkened and withdrawn from the people, instead of popularized and made clear to them. It needs no special interest in the proletarian-democratic society to know that this is a misfortune. But for those who are interested in that society, it is a misfortune of special political importance. For animistic mysteries have always been employed by an aristocracy to befuddle the masses, and the moment the danger arises of a " revolutionary " aristocracy—a danger which only fools will deny—this materialistic animism stands ready to do its work. That Dialectic Universe, which is producing with such an obscure and unquestionable necessity the welfare of the toiling masses, will be found residing in the private chambers of those chosen by history to understand " the art of operating with ideas ", which is " not inborn, and not bestowed with ordinary everyday consciousness ".

It is absolutely necessary that this metaphysical nonsense should be abandoned, and abandoned whole-sale, and without paying any attention to the attempts of academical-old Marxian minds to preserve the pieces of it. Aside entirely from the problem of bureaucratism, the hopes of a revolutionary civilization stand or fall with the true education of the children. And true education can only be founded upon a true psychology. The instinctive position of Lenin in Russia was that of a " fraternal teacher of the people "—to recall again the eloquence of Bakunin—and in that he furnishes an example to all revolutionary leaders that shall follow. him. But in order to develop the full implication of that example, it is necessary to go beyond Lenin. It is necessary to understand how you think, and teach that, as well as the result of it, to those who follow you. It may be that a psychological science would have made little difference in the political wisdom of Lenin ; that locomotive genius had small need of self-analysis. But if Lenin had been conscious of his own intellectual method and position, he might have tapped an immense reservoir of revolutionary will and energy existing in sincere but immature minds, Left Socialist-revolu-tionaries and anarchists, whom he was compelled to dismiss as " revolutionary adventurers ", because he did not know how to teach them. It is no accident that anarchism finds its best adherents among the French and southern European races, who love hard clear thoughts and prefer doubt to metaphysical consolation. Hegelian Marxism will never get a firm foothold in those countries. Any natural child of Montaigne or Machiavelli will always rather remain in a state of innocence than go to school to a German metaphysician. Approach an anarchist, not with the proposition that you know just what the universe is doing, having learned it from a Hegelian philosopher, but with the proposition that a great undertaking requires a great plan, and you have some chance of teaching him how to think. . . .

Moreover if Lenin had understood his own thinking he could have left in his place a body of men better trained to carry it forward than those he has left—condemned to the vain effort to reconcile his wisdom with an antique animistic intellectualism which he ignored and trampled on from the beginning of his life to the end. They would not be trying to explain his powerful rebellion against Marxism as the mere " reflection " of a new historical epoch, or imagining that they can solve by " seeking for contradictions in capitalism " the problems which he solved by seeking in the whole world for nothing but opportunities to do what he wanted to do.

And finally, if Marxism had existed in the consciousness of the Bolsheviks in the form of a science and not a philosophy, the Commissariat of Education in Soviet Russia would present a more thoroughly and systematically revolutionary picture than it does. Never before have so many modern educative ideas been adopted on a large scale as in Soviet Russia ; never have so many bold experiments in scientific education been made. And yet they have been made under the tolerance, rather than by the initiative, of the Bolshevik dictatorship. And that, it seems to me, is an inevitable consequence of the Hegelian-Marxian philosophy. So long as the very preservation of the dictatorship is erroneously identified with the promulgation of a set of ideas hostile to all psychological understanding, a thorough and

systematic revolutionizing of education is impossible.
So long as the proletarian party issues pamphlets indoc-
trinating its members, on pain of exclusion, with a belief
that the sentence " Workers of the world, unite ! " is
not an exhortation to action, but " a reflection in the
heads of Marxists of the fact of proletarian solidarity ",
it is impossible to teach even grammar, to say nothing
of teaching the true art of thinking and being a man.
If " Workers of the world, unite ! " means that the
workers are united, what does " The workers are united "
mean ?

The example is typical of many absurd pronuncia-
mentoes that are put out in the name of education by the
Doctors of the State Philosophy in Soviet Russia. And
it shows, only a little more clearly than usual, the essential
motive of this, as of other philosophies—to convince the
believer that the objective world is at one with his aspiration. To me the most unsatisfactory feature of the
revolutionary experiment in Russia so far, is the failure to
establish a great system of education. They have established in the place of it this great solemn fetish of dialectic
materialism, which is nothing but the old shoes of the
Almighty God.

CHAPTER XII

POST-REVOLUTIONARY UTOPIANISM

A FINAL enemy which the science of revolution will have to conquer is the post-revolutionary utopianism of Marx's own theory. Marx's science of revolution was a practical and realistic scheme only up to, and including, the establishment of a dictatorship of the proletariat which should expropriate the capitalists. The problems arising after that, Marx was inclined to regard, not as postponed problems greater in their complexity than that of capturing the power, but as problems which " history " would solve. The very science of Marxism, indeed, was supposed to begin to die of contradiction and give place to a " higher unity ", when this necessary process of which it was a reflection, had been achieved. Marx's attitude to the subsequent course of history was therefore hardly distinguishable from the general attitude of the utopians. He believed that truly miraculous things would follow of themselves. That there might be a problem of preserving the new society, and preventing its relapse into capitalism, never occurred to his mind.

The principal miracle which Marx anticipated from the social revolution, was a wholesale change in human nature. Marxism knows nothing of the distinction between hereditary instincts and acquired characters. That human nature in its fundamental and general outlines could only be changed by an extended process of selective breeding, whether artificial or natural, is a point that Marx never learned from Darwin, and that he could not learn without breaking down his whole philosophy of history. For that philosophy requires that human nature should be regarded as a mere function of the evolution of the productive forces, an indefinitely variable factor. "The whole of history," Marx tells us, "is nothing but a continual transformation of human nature." And Plekhanov develops this essential thesis of Marxism as follows :

"According to the character of the means of production, men enter into such and such relations in the process of production (since this is a social process), and according to their *relations* in the social process of production, *their habits, their sentiments, their tastes, their way of thinking and acting, in short their nature* is modified. Thus it is not human nature which explains the historic movement, it is the historic movement which fashions human nature in different ways."

From this it follows that once an economic revolution is achieved and completed, the transformation of human nature necessary to sustain it will automatically follow. The problem of adjusting the forms of the new society to the original nature of man does not and cannot exist. Psychology as a science of human behaviour, has no more place in Marxism than psychology as a science of the mind. In building a model hen-house a Marxian would have the good sense to consider the instinctive nature of the hens, but in building an ideal social structure for mankind, he is prevented by his religion from even asking a question about the natural tendencies of this animal.

The extent of the utopian dreaming which has been founded upon this myth of the indefinite changeability of human nature, may be seen in the following assertion of Engels :

" Socialism will abolish both architecture and barrow-pushing as professions, and the man who has given half an hour to architecture will also push the cart a little until his work as an architect is again in demand. It would be a pretty sort of socialism which perpetuated the business of barrow-pushing."

Here it is evident that Engels is not a practical engineer, considering the problem of actually producing a socialist society and making it work. He is a dreamer, discoursing about an ideal state of things which must come in due course, if the universe continues its " endless ascending from the lower to the higher ".

The indifference of Marx and Engels, and of all Marxians, toward the all-important problem of controlling population, is another example of the utopianism inherent in their religion. The population of Soviet Russia is already increasing at the estimated annual rate of 178 for every 10,000 inhabitants, although the total wealth-production of the country is still only 71 per cent. of the pre-war level. Any practical person can see the need of directive intelligence here. For my part, I believe that a free and real human society will never be created by a people who ignore the necessity for intelligent control of the quantity, if not indeed in a negative way the quality, of the population. But it is very difficult for Marxians to see this problem or approach it with practical intelligence, because population is one of those things which are supposed to be especially in the divine care of the Process of Production.

A similar utopianism prevails among Marxians in regard to the problem of sex equality. Seeing that the dependence of woman is largely economic, and that her general independence, like that of man, can be attained only in a proletarian democratic society, they jump to the conclusion that the proletarian revolution will automatically solve the problem of woman's independence. This great achievement, too, they leave in the hands of the Productive Forces. But if you face the actual psychological and physiological elements of the woman's problem, it is only too obvious that it will not be solved automatically, even by a social revolution. It will be solved by men and women, and particularly women who devote their utmost intelligence and energy to its solution.

Another example of the Marxian utopianism, is the theory of the automatic " dying away " of the state. The fact underlying this theory is that most states are in large part, and especially in those parts which make them a nuisance to people who want to make human life beautiful and live it well, an instrument used by the possessing class to defend their vested interest in the existing system, and keep an exploited class in order. Once this system of class exploitation is abolished, and the state takes the form of an association of producers, it can be deprived of its predominant function of repression and inhibition. Its chief service in that direction, at least, will be to prevent a recrudescence of the old system. Nobody can prescribe the limit to which human society might go in the direction of real liberty, once the chief obstacle of class exploitation were removed. But nobody who is deeply interested in liberty, would place an ultimate reliance upon that automatic and all too dialectic " dying away " of the state, which forms a part of the Marxian post-revolutionary utopianism.

A mature science of revolution would replace all such intellectual legends with a direct and simple purpose —a purpose to *see to it* that the proletarian dictatorship and the collective ownership of the means of production shall create, *to the full extent possible at any stage of its development*, a free and true human society. **An** absence of that direct and simple purpose, is to my mind the second most unsatisfactory feature of the Bolshevik experiment in Russia. Wholesale curtailments of liberty and violations of their own ultimate ideal of social relations, are a necessary and intrinsic part of the plan of action of all scientific revolutionists. But revolutionists who imagine that their plan of action is a " natural process " by which the material universe is itself achieving liberty and producing ideal social relations in an indefinite future, will almost inevitably be callous and irresponsible in transgressing liberties and violating social relations in the present. They will be prone to put the means in the place of the end, to ignore the most simple and obvious demands that their own ultimate purpose would put upon them. There is no tyrant so extreme and irresponsible as the virtuous one, who has convinced himself that he is an instrument of the will of God. And this same extremism and irresponsibility of the religious tyrant is to be found, dressed in the guise of revolutionary virtue, in more than one of those Russian Marxists who have convinced themselves that they are the instruments of a Dialectic Universe. They have exceeded the demands of practical necessity in postponing and transgressing their own ultimate purpose. And they have neglected certain simple measures which would seem most obvious to a revolutionist knowing that his purpose is his own, and that he and not history is responsible for its achievement. To what extent this may be a result of inexperience and the complexities of politics and human nature, and to what extent it is attributable to the animistic religion of Marxism, is of course a problem. But it is a problem whose solution demands first of all and most emphatically that this animistic religion should be exposed and abolished.

Lenin himself least of all Marxists was inclined to lean upon " history ", or to leave to that dialectic universe in which he tried to believe the tasks and responsibilities that belonged to him. And yet Lenin was not entirely free from the utopianism inherent in the dialectic philosophy, as the following quotations will show :

" Capitalism inevitably leaves, as an inheritance to Socialism, on the one hand old professional and craft differences . . . and on the other trade unions, which only very slowly and in the course of years can and will develop into broader industrial rather than craft organizations. . . . These industrial unions will in their turn lead to the abolition of the division of labour between people, to the education, training and preparation of workers who will be able to do *everything*."

" Under socialism *all* will take a turn at administration, and will soon become accustomed to the idea of no administration at all."

These statements have no support whatever in the facts of human nature. Only by completely ignoring the data of psychology, and putting a completely metaphysical faith in the place of this science, is it possible for a moment to believe them. Bertrand Russell, whom Lenin could dismiss from the standpoint of revolutionary method as an extreme utopian, has a far more realistic and practical approach than Lenin to this future problem.

" People will be taught," he says, " not only as at present, one trade, or one small portion of a trade, but several trades, so that they can vary their occupation according to the seasons and the fluctuations of demand. Every industry will be self-governing as regards all its internal affairs, and even separate factories will decide for themselves all the questions that only concern those who work in them. There will not be capitalist management, as at present, but management by elected representatives. . . ."

The contrast between these two statements is a contrast between practical possibilities and utopian dreams.

And because they are problems of the future, it is the anarchistic utopian who is practical, and the " scientific socialist " who is dreaming.

Lenin was not affected in his practical character and activity by these dreams, because he knew how to keep them in the remote future. He used to recall his followers to the immediate task, and illustrate the practical-scientific realism with which it should be attacked, by means of the figure of a man who is pulling himself hand-over-hand along a chain. It is not enough, he would say, to believe in the ultimate goal of the historic process—one must be able to " find in the chain at each moment the link which it is necessary to seize with all one's force, in order to retain the chain as a whole and pass to the next link ". There is a difficulty in imagining this picture. It really illustrates better than anything else the absurdity of mixing animistic faith with practical science. For if future history is a chain securely attached to the co-operative commonwealth, there is hardly more than one link within reach, and that is the next one. But this confused figure enabled Lenin to keep the millennium out of the present task, and that is what he used it for. There was perhaps a moment, just after the October revolution, when his faith in the purposes of " history " introduced an element of legend into his practical calculations. Trotsky tells us, at least, that in the early meetings of the Soviet of People's Commissars, Lenin continually asserted that " in six months we will have socialism ". Only four of those six months had passed, however, when Lenin stated at a convention of his party that " The bricks are not yet baked with which socialism will be built."

" What socialism will be when it attains finished forms, we do not know and we cannot say . . . Our programme is a description of what we have begun to do, and of the next steps which we want to take. . . . The name of our party signifies clearly enough that we are going toward complete communism, that we present to ourselves such an abstract proposition as that each will work according to his abilities, and receive according to his needs, without any military control or violence. But it is early to talk about that. When has any state yet begun to die away ? "

What had begun to die away here, was the post-revolutionary utopianism of the Marxian metaphysics. It will inevitably die away in honest minds when the real facts arrive. And the most important question we have to ask is : What shall take its place ? The remarks of Lenin make clear the answer : A thoroughly experimental procedure. The aim will be defined at first very loosely and " abstractly ", and held subject to redefinition in the light of the developing facts ; the facts will be defined more exactly, but they also will be continually redefined in their relation to the aim and the redefinition of it ; and the hypothesis, the plan of action, will be kept in a state of development and living relevance both to the facts and to the aim. In other words doubt will be given its due place, and thought will be used as it was formed to be used in the long process of its evolution.

Marx himself gave a hint of this practical scientific attitude, when he defined communism as " The declaration of a permanent revolution, a class-dictatorship of the proletariat as the necessary transition step to the abolition of class distinctions in general." Here communism does not appear as a neat metaphysical legend—a " negation of the negation " of individual ownership involved in the " capitalist system "—but as a goal of effort loosely defined, and a practical method for going towards it. This definition does not pretend to determine in advance the concrete forms to be assumed by a class-free society, the degree and kind of co-operation and competition which may prove possible or desirable there. Many such questions can only be answered by the experiment itself. What we know in advance is that a sufficient block of the controlling industries must be socialized by the proletariat, so as to assure its dictatorship and the continuance of the experiment. The " declaration of a permanent revolution " implies this. It preserves the extremeness and inflexibility of the purpose, but it leaves open the field of experiment and political invention. It does not deny the complexities of the problem, nor pretend to a knowledge of what cannot be known. It abandons the last remnants of the dialectic philosophy, and therewith the last remnants of utopianism. It presents the revolution as a purpose rather than a belief, and the Marxist as a scientific engineer of revolution.

NOTES AND REFERENCES

NOTES AND REFERENCES

MY notes were composed after the completion of the book, and I urge the reader to ignore them until he understands my thesis as a whole. They discuss certain points which do not belong to a simple statement of the thesis, but would quickly arise in a discussion of it. And they contain translations of certain passages to which I allude in foreign books.

The references are a little unsystematic, and they may also contain inaccuracies, because I have been reading Marxism in various parts of the world, and in different languages, and many of the books to which I refer were not at hand when I prepared my manuscript for the press. All the translations, except where a definite reference is given to the contrary, are my own.

PAGE 14.

" Some such conception " : I try to refrain from dogmatizing in this chapter, and from giving too much expression to my individual opinions. I believe that a tendency toward conscious experience for its own sake will enter into any ultimate explanation of mental evolution (see my article on " The Will to Live " in the " Journal of Philosophy, Psychology and Scientific Methods ", Vol. XIV, No. 4). But psychology is a very immature science, and therefore a great field for individual speculations. I have tried to confine myself to describing the general view of conscious thought which is held by the most advanced investigators in this field, or which, even if it is not consciously held by them, is implied in their investigations.

The reader who wishes to find his way into the literature of the subject, might begin by reading " Genetic Psychology ", by Edwin A. Kirkpatrick, Köhler's " The Mentality of Apes ", John Dewey's " How we Think ", and " The Influence of Darwin ", Freud's " Introduction " to Psycho-analysis, Tansley's " The New Psychology ", Koffka's " The Growth of the Mind ", and L. L. Thurstone's " The Nature of Intelligence ".

Those who think that the instrumental or Darwinian approach to Logic is a purely American phenomenon, should read Vaihinger's book " The Philosophy of ' As If ' ", recently translated into English, but written in Germany in 1877. Vaihinger's philosophy begins with this simple statement : " The object of the world of ideas as a whole is not the portrayal of reality—this would be an utterly impossible task—but rather to provide us with an instrument for finding our way about more easily in the world."

PAGE 18.

" Affirmative scepticism " : I insert these words not because I want to burden the passage of time with another " ism ", but because I want to avoid a possible confusion of my viewpoint with the philosophy of William James, which he called " pragmatism ". Every new development in science is seized upon by animistic minds, and made the basis of a new pretence at metaphysical knowledge. The mind of James was animistic, and he not only contributed to the development of a functional science of psychology, but also tried to make this science the basis of a new kind of metaphysics. His metaphysics is superior to others, in my opinion, only in that it is more easily refuted. His identification of the meaning of ideas with their results in action, is obviously a limitation of the meaning of ideas, and an endorsement of the methods of applied science—definition in terms of specific action, and concrete experimental verification—as the only means of distinguishing true from false meanings. With any animistic idea that he likes very much, however, James forgets that his conception of meaning is a limitation ; he forgets the necessity for defining meanings in terms of specific action, and verifying their truth by concrete experiment. He permits himself to imagine that such ideas are proven true because in a general way, to people like him at least, they are " satisfactory ". Thus he preserves philosophy in its most naïve form, upon the basis of a definition of " meaning " which, if taken seriously, is a death-blow to philosophy.

PAGE 19.

Marx's " Theses on Feuerbach ", translated into English by Austin Lewis, may be found in Engel's " Feuerbach, the Roots of the Socialist Philosophy ". I have not relied, however, upon these translations.

To see how closely these theses anticipated the " Darwinian " view of Intelligence, compare Marx's statement about the nature of sensation, and about the new task of philosophy, with the corresponding statements of John Dewey in his " Reconstruction in Philosophy " :

" The senses lose their place as gateways of knowing, and take their rightful place as stimuli to action." " Philosophy, unless it is to undergo a complete break with the authorized spirit of science, must also alter its nature; it must become operative and experimental."

It is needless for anyone who discusses the influence of the Darwinian view-point upon the development of a scientific logic, to express his obligation to John Dewey. I think Dewey's contribution is most clearly summarized in this book " Reconstruction in Philosophy ", and I recommend it to my reader—along with his " Studies in Experimental Logic "—as extremely important.

I cannot refrain from observing, however, that this book, like other works of these who accept the name of " Pragmatist ", is a little half-hearted in drawing its conclusions. Dewey makes it clear in his first chapter that the original and prevailing function of philosophy has been to prevent practical scientific intelligence from getting hold of the social problem. At least so I read what he says. And in developing this theme he demonstrates the unreality of most of the pretended problems of philosophy. This prepares me to see practical-scientific intelligence get hold of the social problem ! But no, in answer to those who are " at a loss to know what would be left for philosophy " Dewey says : " Would not the elimination of these problems permit philosophy to devote itself to a more fruitful and more needed task ? Would it not encourage philosophy to face the great social and moral defects from which humanity suffers, to concentrate its attention upon clearing up the causes and the exact nature of these evils, and upon developing a clear idea of better social possibilities . . . ? " If this means anything, it means that since philosophers can no longer defend the existing social order by pretending to " know " a superior " reality ", they may still do so by bringing the glamour and authority of the mere name of philosophy into the field of social and political science. Otherwise why not suggest that " philosophers " devote themselves, say, to the more fruitful and more needed task of clearing up the defects in Ford motors ? The real conclusion of Dewey's book, as I read it, would be : If you are seriously interested in removing " the great moral and social defects from which humanity suffers ", inscribe the word *science* on your banner, and beware of every man who speaks to you in the name of philosophy.

Thus Dewey, in his moralistic way, arrives at a position not dissimilar to that of James. Having spent his life in building up a science capable of dealing the death-blow to philosophy, he devotes some further efforts to trying to revive the victim.

I do not doubt that philosophy will revive. It has been knocked out five times before in its short history. But I doubt if it will revive in its full strength of glory. The scepticism of past ages was, as Sextus Empiricus said, like a purge—it carried itself off along with everything else. But the scepticism that rests upon a scientific understanding of the mind that creates systems of belief, is of a more permanent nature. The statement that all truth is a practical definition and interpretation of concrete facts, does not make an exception of itself. It is itself a practical definition and interpretation of concrete mental facts. It destroys the validity of philosophies, but retains its own validity, because it is not a philosophy, but an applied science of the mind.

PAGE 20.

The quotations are from Hegel's " Philosophy of Mind " (Wallace's translation, p. 208) and from his volume on " Logic " in the " Encyclopedia of the Philosophical Sciences ", pp. 47 and 50. (All my references to these two books are to William Wallace's translation.)

PAGE 21.

The quoted phrase is from the following passage in Hegel's " Logic " (p. 18): " The mind or spirit, when it is sentient or perceptive, finds its object in something sensuous ; when it imagines, in a picture or image ; when it wills in an aim or end. But in contrast to, or it may be only in distinction from, these forms' of its existence and of its objects, the mind has also to gratify the cravings of its highest and most inward life. That innermost self is thought. Thus the mind renders thought its object. In the best meaning of the phrase, it comes to itself, for thought is its principle and its very unadulterated self."

PAGE 23.

" Engels describes the ' rapture ' " : " Ludwig Feuerbach und der Ausgang der Klassischen Deutschen Philosophie ", I.

" Dynamic principle " : " Das energische Prinzip ". The phrase is from Marx's own earlier work on the philosophy of Democritus. The biographer is Franz Mehring—ch. V, sec. 1, of his " Karl Marx ".

PAGE 24.

" Hegel himself said " : " Logic ", p. 18.

PAGE 25.

" Desultory empirical observations " : The student should examine Section 81 of Hegel's " Logic " (p. 147 in Wallace's trans-

lation) ; then the chapter on " Dialectic " in Engels' " Landmarks of Scientific Socialism " (A translation of the substance
of his " Herrn Eugen Dühring's Umwälzung der Wissenschaft,"
called " Anti-Dühring " for short) ; and then if possible a
letter written by Engels to Konrad Schmidt on November 1,
1891. This will be enough to convince him that the dialectic
" law of motion " is not a definable and verifiable empirical
generalization, or anything remotely approaching it. Starting
with the assertion that " Everything that surrounds us may be
viewed as an instance of Dialectic ", Hegel proceeds to tell us
about some sufficiently peculiar matters in which we can find
" illustrations " of it, and " traces of its presence ". Here are
two of them : " In political life, as everyone knows, extreme
anarchy and extreme despotism naturally lead to one another."
" The perception of Dialectic in the province of individual
ethics is seen in the well-known adages, Pride comes before a
fall : Too much wit outwits itself." Engels in his " Anti-
Dühring " adds some equally casual illustrations from the sphere
of chemistry and mathematics, and in his letter to Konrad
Schmidt, who was trying to convince himself of the dialectic
philosophy, he makes the following suggestion (I translate
from a Russian text) :

" You as a bridegroom will find a clear model of the insepara-
bility of identity and difference in yourself and your bride. It
is absolutely impossible to determine whether sexual love is
a joy in the fact that there is identity in difference, or that there
is difference in identity. Throw out the difference (in this case
sex) or the identity (the humanity of both) and what have you
left ? "—which shows a remarkable innocence of the varieties
of sexual experience, but will certainly not pass for science
in these days.

Such illustrations of an aphorism parading as proofs of a
law, would not have convinced anybody even in Hegel's time.
For convincing people, the dialectic philosophy relied entirely
upon *rationalistic* devices, of which two examples will suffice.
One of them is the difficulty about making physical motion
seem logical—the paradox, or conundrum, discovered by
Zeno. I have discussed it in my chapter on " The Dialectic
Method ", p. 107. The other consists of building up a great
mystification about the general idea of " being ". You arrive
at general ideas by dropping out of your connotation the concrete
and real attributes of things, and when you arrive at " being ",
the most general idea which is possible, you find that all the
attributes are gone, and the idea really *means nothing* ! This
may amuse you a little, but it will soon strike you as more
interesting to think about *something.* . . . That is a simple

and natural, and also in the rough state a *scientific* way of stating the principal fact upon which Hegel builds up his dialectic mystification. I will quote his own words in " The Science of Logic ", Part I, Ch. I. (Here I have to take the responsibility for the translation.)

" A.—BEING.

" Being, pure· being—without further definition. In its undefined immediacy it is only equal to itself, and also is not unequal compared with anything else, has no distinction within itself, nor without. By any definition or content, which might be distinguished in it, or through which it might be put in distinction to something else, it would fail to be grasped in its purity. It is pure undefinedness and emptiness.—There is nothing to contemplate in it, if one can speak here of contemplating, or it is only this pure empty contemplation itself. There is likewise nothing to think in it, or it is just only this empty thought. Being, the undefined immediate, is in fact nothing, and neither more nor less than nothing.

" B.—NOTHING.

" Nothing, pure nothing ; it is simple equality to itself, complete emptiness, absence of definition and content ; undistinguishedness in itself.—In so far as contemplation or thought can be mentioned here, it is considered a distinction, whether something or nothing is contemplated or thought. To contemplate or think nothing has thus a meaning ; the two are distinguished, thus nothing is (exists) in our contemplation or thought ; or rather it is empty contemplation and thought itself ; and the same empty contemplation or thought as pure being.—Nothing is consequently the same definition, or rather lack of definition, and thus the same in general as pure Being.

" C.—BECOMING.
" *The Unity of Being and Nothing.*

" Pure being and pure nothing are just the same. What the truth is, is neither being or nothing, but the fact that being —not passes over—but has passed over into nothing, and nothing into being. But in the same way the truth is, not their undistinguishedness, but that they are not the same, that they are absolutely different, but nevertheless undivided and indivisible, and each immediately vanishes in its opposite. Their truth is, thus, this motion of immediate vanishing of one in the other ; becoming ; a motion in which both are distinguished, but through a distinction, which itself has just now immediately been dissolved."

The most significant passage in Hegel's " Logic ", for those who understand the practical functions of the mind, is that in which he cautions the reader against taking the statement that " being and nothing are the same " for a joke (" Logic ", p. 163). It is a joke, in the most technical sense of the term—although it is not a very good one—and a functional logic would have no disposition to take it in any other way. (See my " Sense of Humour ", III and IV.)

" Marx himself used to describe " : See the preface to the second edition of " Das Kapital ".

PAGE 26.

" First taste of Hegel " : Mehring, " Karl Marx ", II, 1.

" As he once contemplated doing " : See his letter to Engels, January 14, 1858.

PAGE 27.

Lafargue : " Le Déterminisme Économique de Karl Marx ".

Plekhanov : " As to the question of the Development of a Monistic View of History ", p. 103 of the Soviet edition. " In order to escape from ignorance covered up in a more or less learned terminology, we must pass from the study of human nature to a study of the nature of social relations."

Kautsky · " Karl Marx and his Historical Significance ", II. In an essay on " Social Instinct in Marx and Darwin ", Kautsky does broach the question of the relation between genetic psychology and Marxism, but only to remark that this science corroborates the " Theses on Feuerbach ".

Lenin : In quoting a passage from Engels' " Feuerbach ", Lenin translates the German words " Gedanken-Abbilder " as " mental photographs ". " Things which seem changeless, and likewise ideas, their mental photographs made by the head, are in a state of continuing change " (" Karl Marx, A Short Biographical Essay with an Exposition of Marxism ", p. 13). In his " Materialism and Empiro-Criticism ", Lenin makes the following similar statements :
" Matter is a philosophic category for the designation of an objective reality, which is given to man in his *sensations*, which is copied, photographed, reflected by our sensations, existing independently of them " (p. 142 of the first edition). " Materialism

in general recognizes an objectively real existence (matter) independent of the *consciousness, sensation, experience,* etc., of humanity. Historic materialism recognizes a social existence independent of the *social consciousness* of humanity. Consciousness in both cases is only a reflection of existence, at the best an approximately true (adequate, mentally exact) reflection of it " (p. 394). " A recognition of the objective orderedness of nature, and the approximately true reflection of this order *in the head of man* is materialism " (p. 175). " To recognize the necessity of nature and infer from it the necessity of *thought* is materialism " (p. 189). " *Knowledge* can be biologically useful . . . only in case it reflects an objective reality, not dependent upon man " (p. 155).

I give these different quotations with my own italics, in order to show the complete lack of psychological science, or the conception of such a thing, in Lenin's mind. " Sensation ", " thought", " consciousness", " social consciousness ", " knowledge ", " experience ", " ideas "—any names that happen to occur to him for anything that exists or takes place " in the head of man "—are lumped together without examination or discrimination as automatic photographs of the material environment. This is not materialistic philosophy ; it is mere negligence of psychological facts and distinctions. Lenin's " materialism " is satisfied by his assertion that " matter, nature, existence, the physical, is primary, and spirit, consciousness, sensation, the psychical, is secondary " (p. 164)—a statement which seems to him, because he has no conception of a psychological science, practically interchangeable with these other statements.

PAGE 28.

" Consciousness in general " : " Materialism and Empiro-Criticism ", p. 391. The other quotation is from " The Significance of Militant Materialism ", an article contributed by Lenin to an early number of " Pod Znamenem Marxisma ", a Monthly Journal of Philosophy and Social Economy established by the Bolsheviks after the revolution.

K. Kornilov : " Dialectic Method in Psychology ", and " Contemporary Psychology and Marxism ", articles in " Pod Znamenem Marxisma ", 1923 and 1924. An entire text-book has been written by a communist in Orenburg, V. Ia. Struminsky, entitled : " Psychology : An Attempt to Expound the Fundamental Principles of Scientific Psychology from the Point of View of Dialectic Materialism ". The book has little value, both because Struminsky's psychology is old-fashioned, and because he caters to the State Religion. He thinks it necessary to prove that Marx himself, whatever may be the failings of his followers, was a great and perfect psychologist.

PAGE 30.

The phrases quoted are all from Hegel's " Logic " (pp. 50, 51, 149).

PAGE 31.

" Hegel had the same phobia " : " Logic ", p. 69 : " One word on the relation of rational to empirical psychology," he says. " The former, because it sets itself to apply thought to cognize mind and even to demonstrate the result of such thinking, is the higher ; whereas empirical psychology starts from perception, and only recounts and describes what perception supplies." In short it only tells us the facts !

Hegel pretends to study an evolution of the mind, but it is in reality a resurrection of God that he is studying. It is a coming back to its " true and unadulterated self " of his *rationalistic conception* of the mind, after having been " alienated from itself " in matter. Such a study of its genesis obviously does not, and cannot, affect the conception. Hegel's attitude to a real genetic psychology may be inferred from the fact that he begins his " Encyclopedia of the Philosophical Sciences " by making a fixed distinction between man and the animals upon the ground that man " thinks ", and he recurs to it ten times in the first one hundred pages. His " Lectures on the Philosophy of Religion " begin with the same assertion : " It is through thought . . . or more definitely, it is by reason of his being Spirit, that man is man."

PAGE 33.

" Socrates " : " Although Socrates was doubtless sincerely interested in the reconciliation of the two sides, yet the fact that he approached the matter from the side of matter-of-fact method . . . was enough to bring him to the condemnation of death as a contemner of the gods and a corrupter of youth." John Dewey, " Reconstruction in Philosophy ", p. 14. In connection with this chapter read also Thorstein Veblen's essay on " The Evolution of the Scientific Point of View ".

PAGE 35.

" The true reason world " : Hegel's " Logic " (pp. 152, 153).

PAGE 36.

" Marx's childhood was less churchly-religious " : At the age of nineteen Engels wrote as follows : " I pray every day ;

almost all day long I pray that the truth may be given me.
I have done this ever since doubts assailed me, but still I cannot return to our faith . . . I write these lines with tears in
my eyes, it is hard for me to control my emotion, but nevertheless I feel that I will not be lost, that I will find God, toward
whom I aspire with all my heart." (I translate from a Russian
text given by Riazanov, " Essays on the History of Marxism ",
p. 36.)

" Doctor's Thesis " : " The General Differences between
the Nature Philosophies of Democritus and Epicurus ", written
in 1841. (" Aus dem literarischen Nachlass von Karl Marx,
Friedrich Engels und Ferdinand Lasalle, herausgegeben von
Franz Mehring ", vol. I, p. 65.)

PAGE 37.

" And that faith in the omnipotence of the Idea " : The
quotation is from " Schelling and Revelation : A Criticism
of the Latest Reactionary Attempt upon the Free Philosophy "—
a pamphlet long attributed to Bakunin, but written by Engels,
and published in 1842. (From the Russian text given by
Riazanov, " Essays on the History of Marxism ", pp. 40, 41.)

PAGE 38.

" Says Marx " : In " Herr Vogt ". Compare also the
following statement of Marx in the correspondence published
in the " Deutsch-Französische Jahrbucher ", in 1843 : " We
will not then oppose the world like doctrinaires with a new
principle . . . We expose new principles to the world out of
the principles of the world itself. . . . We explain to it only
the real object for which it struggles, and consciousness is a
thing it must acquire even though it objects to it."

PAGE 39.

" By means of all seeming accidents " : The phrases quoted
are from Engels' " Feuerbach ", IV and I. It should be
remembered that before sending this book to the press Engels
re-read a manuscript on " German Ideologies " written jointly
by him and Marx in 1845-46, an enormous and wearisome
book in which, as Marx said later, they " settled accounts "
with their " own former philosophical views ". " We submitted
the manuscript to the gnawing criticism of the mice, and this
the more willingly that our own chief end was achieved—we
had arrived at an understanding between ourselves." Engels'
" Anti-Dühring ", the other exposition of the philosophy of
Dialectic Materialism, was read over in manuscript by Marx
himself. Thus it is admissible to attribute to Marx all the
essential philosophic ideas expressed by Engels.

" It was not because of emotional dependence " : I say this with so much assurance, because of the paragraph in Engels' " Feuerbach ", where he mentions in the most casual manner the scientific prediction of an end of life on the earth, and the probability that there is, therefore, " in human history not only an ascending but also a descending branch ". In the face of this probability—which is an emotional, if not indeed an intellectual, reduction to absurdity of the whole philosophy of " an endless evolutionary progress of human society from the lower to the higher "—Engels nonchalantly remarks : " We find ourselves, at any rate, still at a considerable distance from the turning-point, where the history of society begins to go downward. . . ."

" Being a German philosopher " : I mean, *Being a German philosopher of the classical or official tradition.* Schopenhauer was a German philosopher, and Schopenhauer first perceived that relation between impulse and intelligence which lies at the basis of modern psychology. But Schopenhauer was not an official German philosopher ; he was not an " instructor of youth appointed by the state ". Nietzsche perceived the significance of this fact. Nietzsche was far more Marxian than Marx in his attitude to the official German philosophy. " Experience teaches us," he said, " that nothing stands so much in the way of developing great philosophers as the custom of supporting bad ones in state universities. . . . It is the popular theory that the posts given to the latter make them ' free ' to do original work ; as a matter of fact, the effect is quite contrary. . . . No state would ever dare to patronize such men as Plato and Schopenhauer. And why ? Because the state is always afraid of them. . . . It seems to me that there is need for a higher tribunal outside the universities to critically examine the doctrines they teach. As soon as philosophers are willing to resign their salaries, they will constitute such a tribunal. . . ." (" Schopenhauer als Erzieher ", Translation by H. L. Mencken in " Nietzsche ".)

" The simultaneous occurrence " : I give this " Thesis " in the form found by Riazanov in Marx's note-book, and not as Engels gives it in his " Feuerbach ". (" Essays on the History of Marxism ", p. 75.)

PAGE 40.

Plekhanov : " From Idealism to Materialism ", II.

Rosa Luxemburg : From an article in " Vorwärts " on the twentieth anniversary of Marx's death, cited by Siemkovsky in his " Khrestomatia Marxisma ". (I translate from his Russian text.) In her speech at the Inaugural Congress of the Commu-

nist Party of Germany (Spartacus League) the emotional
function performed by this idea in Rosa Luxemburg's mind,
is even more clear : " On November 10th our revolutionists
allowed to slip from their grasp nearly half the instruments
of power they had seized on November 9th. We learn from
this, on the one hand, that our revolution is subject to the
prepotent law of historical determinism, a law which guarantees
that, despite all difficulties and complications, notwithstanding
all our own errors, we shall nevertheless advance step by step
towards the goal." (British " Communist Review ", September 1921.) Here even the present failure is converted into
an evidence of future success.

PAGE 41.

Plekhanov : " History shows that even fatalism, not only
does not always hinder energetic practical action, but, on the
contrary, in certain epochs has been a psychologically necessary
foundation for such action. In evidence we may cite the
Puritans, surpassing in their energy all other parties in seven-
teenth-century England, and the followers of Mahomet, sub-
jecting to their power in a short space of time an enormous
strip of earth from India to Spain. They are greatly mistaken,
who think that we need only be convinced of the inevitable
arrival of an event of a given kind, in order to lose every psychological possibility of co-operating with or opposing it.

" Here all depends on the question whether my own activity
constitutes a necessary link in the chain of necessary events.
If yes—then so much the less do I waver, so much the more
decisively I act." (" The Question of the Rôle of Personality
in History ", an article contributed by Plekhanov to a Collection entitled " After Twenty Years ".) Plekhanov speaks in
a footnote of Moses and Cromwell. " All Cromwell's activities,"
he says, " were for him coloured in advance with the hue of
necessity. This not only did not prevent him from striving
from victory to victory, but gave to his efforts an unconquerable
power."

PAGE 42.

" The definition of freedom " : Read Sections 145, 46 and
47 of Hegel's " Logic ", and Section B of the second division
of Part II of his " Lectures on the Philosophy of Religion "
(translated by Spiers and Sanderson). And do not read them in
the mood of filial piety that Marxians cherish towards Hegel.
Do not mistake unintelligibility for wisdom. Remember that
Marx too disliked Hegel until he had Hegel drilled into him at
school.

Hegel says : " The link of necessity *qua* necessity is identity, as still inward and concealed, because it is the identity of what are esteemed actual things, although their very self-subsistence is bound to be necessity. The circulation of substance through causality and reciprocity therefore only expressly makes out or states that self-subsistence is the infinite negative self-relation—a relation *negative*, in general, for in it the act of distinguishing and intermediating becomes a primariness of actual things independent one against the other—and *infinite self-relation*, because their independence only lies in their identity.

" This truth of necessity, therefore, is *Freedom*."

Whatever that may mean logically, it is plain that science cannot bother with it, for the simple reason that science has too much to do. And what it means *morally*, and *politically*, Hegel takes pains to make as clear, as his logical meaning is obscure :

" We may note in passing," he says, " how important it is for any man to meet everything that befalls him in the spirit of the old proverb which describes each man as the architect of his own fortune. . . . The other way would be to lay the blame of whatever we experience upon other men, upon unfavourable circumstances, and the like. And this is a fresh example of the language of unfreedom, and at the same time the spring of discontent. If man saw, on the contrary, that whatever happens to him is only the outcome of himself, and that he only bears his own guilt, he would stand free, and in everything that came upon him would have the consciousness that he suffered no wrong. . . . It is their view of necessity, therefore, which is the root of the content and discontent of men."

That is the Marxian doctrine of historic necessity, studied " from the standpoint of its origin ". The meaning of it in plain language is this : " Speculative philosophy is too difficult for you, a simple artisan or perhaps a housekeeper, to understand. But I will tell you ' in passing ' what you would learn from it, if you *could* understand. You would learn that it is right and proper for you to feel ' free '—to feel that your choices are real—so far as taking the whole responsibility for your misfortunes is concerned, but when it comes to doing anything to change your ' circumstances ', then you must recognize that your ' freedom ' is only a consciousness of the necessity of everything's being just what it is."

" One of the most brilliant discoveries " : Quoted from the article by Plekhanov above mentioned.

PAGE 43.

" The thinking of Plekhanov about the doctrine of necessity " : For example the following paragraph from the same article :

" A consciousness of the unconditional necessity of a given phenomenon can only strengthen the energy of the man who favours that phenomenon, and considers himself one of the forces producing it. If such a man should fold his arms, because he is aware of this necessity, he would thereby show that he knows little about arithmetic. Let us suppose that the phenomenon A must necessarily appear, if we have at hand a given sum of conditions S. You have proven to me that this sum of conditions is partly at hand already, and partly will be at hand at a given time T. Convinced of this I—a man favouring the phenomenon A—cry ' How nice that is ! ' and flop down to sleep right up to the joyful day of the event you have foretold. What comes of that ? Just this : In your reckoning, into the sum S, necessary to the accomplishment of the phenomenon A, entered also *my activity*, equal, let us say, to a. Inasmuch as I took my little nap, at the moment T, the sum of conditions favourable to the occurrence of the given phenomenon will now not be S, but S *minus a*, which changes the whole state of affairs."

Any reader who has time to think, will see that if Plekhanov has proven anything here, it is the opposite of what he set out to prove. He has at least given an excellent illustration of the opposite thesis—namely that all practical thought or argument, implies that the future is *not determined*. You have to be able to say " If a man should . . ." and *mean it*, in order to talk sense about a practical problem.

In his preface to a Russian translation of Engels' Socialism Utopian and Scientific, Plekhanov has some more remarks of the same kind :

" The chief distinguishing feature of scientific socialism is now defined for us with complete clarity. Its advocates are not satisfied with the *hope* that the socialist ideals, thanks to their elevated character, will attract general sympathy and therefore triumph. No—they require *certainty* that this very attraction of general sympathy by the socialist ideals is a *necessary social process*. And they derive this certainty from an analysis of contemporary economic relations and the course of their development. . . . Certain writers, for example Stammler, remark that if the triumph of socialism is a historic necessity, then the practical activity of the social-democrats is *entirely superfluous*. Why help to create phenomena which will in any case inevitably appear ? But this is a pitiful and ridiculous sophism. Looking upon historical development from the standpoint of necessity, the social democracy looks upon its own activity as a *necessary link* in the chain of those necessary conditions, the combination of which makes inevitable the

triumph of socialism. A necessary link cannot be *superfluous* :
its removal would break the whole chain of events."

Here again the alternative : *If* my activity is withdrawn,
the whole chain of events will be broken. The only question
then is : Can I, or can I not withdraw my activity ? And
if I can *not*, then what is the use of talking ? What is the use of
thinking ? In a world which contained no genuine alternatives,
thinking would never have arisen.

I give two more quotations from Plekhanov, as there is no
better way to cure practical minds of a taste for Hegelian
Marxism.

" The Marxists have succeeded in finding a bridge uniting
ideals with reality. They have lifted themselves up to Monism.
According to their opinion, capitalism in the course of its own
development leads to its own negation and the realization of
their . . ideals. That is historic necessity. The Marxist
serves as one of the instruments of that necessity, and cannot
fail to serve as such, both because of his social situation, and
because of his mental and moral character, created by this
situation. That also is the side of necessity. But once his social
situation has developed in him just this and not another character, he not only serves as an instrument of necessity, and not
only cannot fail to serve as such, but he passionately desires and
cannot fail to desire to serve. This is the side of freedom, or
more truly, this is freedom identifying itself with necessity
—it is necessity transforming itself into freedom." (" The Rôle
of Personality in History.")

" Engels dedicated his life to an extraordinarily high aim,
the liberation of the proletariat. He also had his ideal, but it
was not everlastingly separated from reality. His ideal was this
same reality, but the reality of to-morrow, a reality which will
come into being, not because Engels was idealistic, but because
the attributes of the present reality are such that out of it,
according to its own inward laws, must develop that reality
of to-morrow, which may be called the ideal of Engels. *Undeveloped* people may ask us : if the whole thing lies in the attributes of reality, then what is the use of Engels ? Why should
he mix into an unavoidable historic process with his ideals ?
Cannot the business get along without him ? From the objective side, the situation of Engels presents itself thus : In the
process of passing from one of its forms to another, reality
seized upon him, as one of the necessary instruments of the
economic overturn. From the subjective side, it results that
to Engels his participation in the historic movement is agreeable,
that he considers this his duty and the great task of his life."
(Remarks upon Engels' book " Ludwig Feuerbach ".)

234 THE SCIENCE OF SOCIAL REVOLUTION

Thus after all the commotion and trumpeting about realism and materialism and atheism, and getting down to the hard business facts, we find ourselves in exactly the same position as the Apostle Paul. We are " seized upon " by an abstract " Reality ", and made to " serve " as its " instruments ", and we find it not only agreeable, but " our duty and the great task of our lives " to serve !

" When Engels says " : " Anti-Dühring ", I, XI

PAGE 45.

" Marx and Engels repudiated " : " Capital ", vol. I, ch. 13, footnote to page 406 of Untermann's translation. " Feuerbach ", II. " Socialism Utopian and Scientific ", p. 38.

PAGE 46.

" The Abolition of Religion " : The quotation is from Marx's " Zur Kritik der Hegelschen Rechtsphilosophie ", published in 1844. (" Nachlass ", vol. I, p. 385.)

" Marx himself declared " : See the Introduction to his " Critique of Political Economy ", published in 1859, and his letter to Lassalle, February 22, 1858. " Hegel," he says in this letter, " first understood the whole history of philosophy, and you cannot demand of him that he should make no mistakes in the details."

Engels made the same two contradictory assertions. In his Introduction to the English edition of " Socialism Utopian and Scientific " (page xxxvii) he declares that philosophical ideas are " offshoots of the economic relations prevailing in a given society ". In his " Anti-Dühring " (the chapter on Dialectic) he asserts that the whole history of philosophy has been an independent dialectical process.

In an " Introduction to the Philosophy of Dialectic Materialism ", by A. Deborin, a book which has reached its third edition in Soviet Russia, we have an explanation of the whole course of modern philosophy as an independent dialectic development. But the author apologizes in his preface for not having *also* explained modern philosophy as a development determined by " social relations at the basis of which lies the evolution of the productive forces " ! Such a double-barrelled history of philosophy seems to Deborin the natural Marxian product, whose only drawback is that it would require " an extended work of several volumes ".

The way in which Marx fell into this inconsistency was undoubtedly as follows : Hegel considered social and political history to be a self-development of the divine Reason in an alien form. Therefore Hegel could describe the history of philosophy as an independent self-development of Reason, and yet at the same time declare that the philosophy of any historic period is a reflection of the social and political history of that period. " It is one Mind," as he says, " which manifests itself in and impresses itself upon these different elements." Marx retained these two ways of viewing the history of philosophy through mere habituation, although his substitution of the forces of production for the Divine Mind as an explanation of history, had rendered them inconsistent. (My quotations here are from Hegel's " Lectures on the History of Philosophy ", Haldane's translation, vol. I, pp. 5 and 115.)

PAGE 47.

The quotation is from the Introduction to Marx's " Critique of Political Economy ". (My own translation.)

PAGE 49.

" The forces of production rebel " : The quotation is from Engel's " Anti-Dühring ", III, II.

PAGE 50.

" *Condition* and *determine* " : The German words are *bedingt* and *bestimmt*. Plekhanov interchanges *condition* and *cause* in the same way : " Social man himself creates his social relations. But if he creates at a given time these and not other relations, this happens, you may be sure, not without a cause ; it is conditioned by the state of the productive forces." (" Rôle of Personality.") Engels, in his original outline for the Communist Manifesto defined communism itself as " the science of the *conditions* of the emancipation of the proletariat ". (My italics.)

That Marx at his most Marxian, really conceives of a positive and detailed causation of the ideological superstructure by the economic basis, may be seen in a footnote in Chapter XIII of the first volume of " Das Kapital ". Here he suggests that one can infer religious ideas from the material relations of the society in which they arise, and that this would be " the only materialistic, and therefore scientific " method of studying religion.

Lafargue : In an essay on " Economics, Natural Science, and Mathematics ".

PAGE 51.

" The Marxian explanation of law and the state " : I believe it is true that this explanation is " usually expressed in a dynamic form " at least by revolutionary Marxists, although in the classical exposition of it the state appears to have arisen out of reasons rather than causes. " The state," Engels says, " is the product of society at a certain stage of its development. The state is tantamount to an acknowledgment that the given society has become entangled in an insoluble contradiction with itself, that it has broken up into irreconcilable antagonisms of which it is powerless to rid itself. And in order that these antagonisms, these classes with their opposing economic interests, may not devour one another and society itself in their sterile struggle, some force standing seemingly above society, becomes necessary so as to moderate the force of their collisions and to keep them within the bounds of ' order '. And this force arising from society, but placing itself above it, which gradually separates itself from it—this force is the state." (" The Origin of the Family, Private Property and the State ", translated by Untermann, ix.)

This explanation is decidedly metaphysical and mystical, but it is usually very quickly supplemented and made real and scientific by adding some such statement as this : " The state is nothing but a machine for the oppression of one class by another " (Engels' Introduction to " The Civil War in France "), or " The state power is nothing but an organization given to themselves by the ruling classes—capitalists and landlords— in order to defend their social privileges " (Engels' Letter to Kuno, January 24, 1872), or, The state is " an organization for the systematic use of violence by one class against another " (Lenin, " State and Revolution ").

Reformists, who wish to make the doctrines of Marx as mild as possible, cling to the metaphysical statement of this theory, and maintain on the basis of it that the state is an organ for the " reconciliation " of opposing class interests. Inasmuch as everything in the world is supposed, according to the dialectic philosophy, to be engaged in the process of reconciling opposites in a higher unity, the reformists have rather the best of this argument, so long as the theory is stated in the metaphysical form. The first three pages of Lenin's book, " State and Revolution ", are therefore occupied with wriggling out of Engels' classical statement, and arriving at the scientific assertion that " The state is an organ of class rule ", which " was created by the governing class ". The whole first chapter of this book is a proof of the inappropriateness and inconvenience to a practical revolutionist of a metaphysical theory of history.

" The religious world " : " Capital ", vol. I, ch. I, sec. IV. This view-point is developed by Engels in the concluding

chapter of his " Anti-Dühring ".   " Religion," he says,
" is nothing but the fantastic reflection in the heads of men of
those earthly powers which rule over their daily life, a reflection
in which earthly powers take on the form of unearthly ones."

Compare with this glib statement James H. Leuba's work on
" The Psychology of Religious Mysticism ".

" Calvin's doctrine of predestination " :   The quotation
is from " Socialism Utopian and Scientific ", Introduction,
p. xxi.   In Engels' " Feuerbach ", IV, Calvinism appears as
" the authentic religious disguise of the *interests* of the contemporary bourgeoisie ".   (My italics.)

In order to realize the remoteness of this sort of thing from
exact science, the reader might compare with Engels' explanation
of the doctrine of predestination, Pokrovsky's explanation of
the doctrine of free will.   Pokrovsky is the author of an excellent
Marxian history of Russia.   Science has proven, he declares,
that all things are in a state of absolutely determined change,
but the bourgeoisie, in order to make their class enemies
believe that the present order of society is an exception to this
rule, have invented the doctrine that man is free from causal
determination !

PAGE 52.

Trotsky : " Literature and Revolution ", IV.

PAGE 54.

" Principle of investigation " :   " Historic Materialism is
not a finished system crowned with unalterable truth.   It
represents simply a scientific method for the investigation of
the human process of development."   Franz Mehring, " Concerning Historic Materialism " (Russian text).

" Our interpretation of life is chiefly an introduction to
study. . . ."   (Engels' Letter to Conrad Schmidt, August 5,
1890.)

" Classical philosophy " :   See Engels' Letter to Conrad
Schmidt, October 27, 1890.   The quotations are from his
" Feuerbach ", V.   See also the concluding chapter where he
speaks of " that great theoretic mind ", that " mind for pure
scientific investigation, indifferent whether the results were
practically profitable or not, contrary to the police regulations
or not ", which had been " the honour of Germany in the
period of her deepest political humiliation ".   A more *un-
Marxian* description of a cultural phenomenon could hardly
be imagined.

Hegel himself clearly perceived and frankly announced the

reactionary and animistic mission of German philosophy in the modern scientific world. " We shall see in the history of philosophy," he said in his inaugural address at Heidelburg, " that in other European countries in which the sciences and the culture of the understanding have been prosecuted with zeal and with respect, Philosophy, excepting in name, has sunk even from memory, and that it is in the German nation that it has been retained as a peculiar possession. We have received the higher call of Nature to preserve this holy flame, just as the Eumolpidæ in Athens had the conservation of the Eleusinian Mysteries, the inhabitants of the island of Samothrace the preservation of a higher divine service. . . ."
How much truer than what Engels says about German philosophy !

" Feudal and Bureaucratic despotism " : The phrase occurs in " Revolution and Counter-Revolution in Germany ", articles by Engels published in the New York Tribune over Marx's name.

PAGE 55.

Plekhanov : " The Rôle of Personality in History." Engels also, and in the same incidental way, acknowledges that an " understanding of the causes of economic and political development and the conditions confronting the revolution " gives us additional assurance of its early success. (Letter to Bebel, December 11, 1884.)

PAGE 56.

Marx : Letter to Kugelmann, April 17, 1871.

PAGE 57.

Engels : Letter to Starkenburg, January 25, 1894.

Hegel : " Logic ", p. 265.

PAGE 58.

Engels : " Feuerbach ", IV.

" Problems which trouble them the most " : A good example of this troubledness may be found in Riazanov's Preface to his excellent " Essays on the History of Marxism ". He makes on the first page the following statement : " One may say— and from the theoretical standpoint it would be correct—that any historic process, or any definite part of it, this or that change in the life of a people, would have taken place without the co-operation of any given historic personality."
Upon the page immediately after that, he makes the following

statement : " One of the most interesting phenomena in world history is the fact that the ' creative power ' of ideas, and the deciding rôle (*sic*) of historic personalities has nowhere appeared so fully as in the lives of the two founders of the materialistic interpretation of history."

Engels : Letter to Starkenburg, January 25, 1894. " If there had been no Napoleon, another would have taken his place. That is proven by the fact that the man was always found as soon as he was needed : Cæsar, Augustus, Cromwell." (Except, we may add, when he was not found : absence at other important moments of Cæsar, Augustus, Cromwell !)

PAGE 59.

Trotsky : Speech at the Ukrainian Communist Party Conference in Kharkov, April 5, 1923, reprinted in his book " About Lenin ".

Kautsky : " What does the Materialistic Interpretation of History Ask, and What Can it Give ? "—one of the articles in his discussion with the English socialist, Belfort Bax, published in " Die Neue Zeit " in 1896. " We ought not to protest against the ' reproach ' that we have leaders. Yes we have leaders, and it depends to a considerable degree upon the qualities of our leaders whether our road to victory will be long or short, whether it will be comfortable or covered with thorns." Engels also speaks of the " end-result " in discussing the manner in which " history " operates (Letter to Joseph Bloch, September 21, 1890).

PAGE 60.

Bernstein : " Die Voraussetzung des Socialismus and die Aufgaben der Sozial-democratie ", translated into English under the title " Evolutionary Socialism ".

Jaurès : I have in mind his debate with Paul Lafargue on the Idealist and Materialist Interpretation of History.

Croce : " Materialismo storico ed economia Marxistica.'

Simkhovitch : " Marxism Versus Socialism."

Seligmann : " The Economic Interpretation of History."

PAGE 61.

Bernstein : " Evolutionary Socialism."

Kautsky : " Bernstein and the Materialist Interpretation of History."

Engels : Letter to Joseph Bloch, September 21, 1890, and to Conrad Schmidt, October 27, 1890. (My translations of the second letter are from a Russian text.)

PAGE 62.

Kautsky : " The Materialistic Interpretation of History and the Psychological Factor "—his first article in the discussion with Belfort Bax, referred to above.

" It was Marx and not history " : That Marx was also a product of history, and his purposes and ideas conditioned by the age and society in which he lived, does not alter this fact or contradict it. We do not know the degree in which Marx's purposive ideas were conditioned by his place in history, and we do not know the positive concrete causes of those ideas at all. We shall never escape from metaphysics without ceasing to pretend to know everything.

PAGE 63.

" Early Christians " : " Delivered from capitalist slavery, from the innumerable horrors, barbarities, absurdities, and infamies of capitalist exploitation, people will gradually *become accustomed* to the observance of those elementary rules of social life, known for ages, and repeated for thousands of years in all maxims, to their observance without violence, without compulsion, without subjection, without the *special apparatus* for compulsion which is called the state " (Lenin, " State and Revolution ", V. 2).

PAGE 65.

" All past history " : A statement often repeated by Marx and Engels and always in this sweeping form. The quotation here is from Engels' " Socialism Utopian and Scientific ", p. 41. The quotation at the end of the chapter is from the Communist Manifesto.

" Penetrated with unity " : The phrase is from the article by Rosa Luxemburg, published in " Vorwärts " on the twentieth anniversary of Marx's death (Russian text, see note to p. 40). " Since Marx established in the sphere of philosophy, history and political economy the historical point of view of the working class, the thread of bourgeois investigations in these spheres has been broken. Natural philosophy, in the classical sense of the word, has ceased to exist. The philosophy of history has come to an end. Scientific political economy has come to an end. In historical investigations wherever an unconscious and inconsistent materialism does not prevail, the place of a complete theory is occupied by a many-coloured eclecticism —that is to say, the idea of an explanation of the historic process penetrated with unity has been renounced, the philosophy of history has been renounced."

PAGE 66.

" The predominating purpose " : My quotations are from Marx's earliest exposition of his social theory, " The Poverty of Philosophy ", II, V, and from his " Zur Kritik des Sozial-democratischen Programms von Gotha ", a letter written late in his life.

PAGE 67.

" Marx greeted Darwin's theory " : Letter to Lassalle, January 16, 1861.

Engels : Introduction to the Communist Manifesto (1888).

" Glorious corroboration " : The phrase of Anton Pannekoek in his " Marxism and Darwinism ", the ablest and most original of all the writings on this subject.

PAGE 68.

" Universal law of motion " : This is in substance Engels' definition of the dialectic both in " Feuerbach " and " Anti-Dühring ".

PAGE 70.

" In studying revolutions " : From the Introduction to the " Critique of Political Economy " (See page 48 of this book).

" The law of development of human history " : The phrase is from Engels' speech at the grave of Karl Marx.

PAGE 71.

" He speaks of his doctrine " : See, for instance, the Preface to the first edition of " Das Kapital ". " My standpoint, which views the development of the economic social formation as a process in natural history, holds the individual responsible less than any other for relations whose creature he remains, no matter how much he may raise himself subjectively above them."

PAGE 72.

" Reflection in thought " : " Socialism Utopian and Scientific ", p. 47.

PAGE 73.

" General expression " : " The theoretical conclusions of the communists . . . merely express in general terms actual relations springing from an existing class struggle, from a historical movement going on under our very eyes." (Communist Manifesto, II.) " The theoretical propositions of the communists are by no means founded on ideas and principles invented or discovered by this or that reformer of the world : they are merely a general expression of the class struggle " (Kautsky—Debate with Belfort Bax).

Rosa Luxemburg : Article in " Vorwärts " on the Twentieth Anniversary of Marx's death. (See note to p. 40.)

PAGE 75.

Lenin : The quotations are from " Materialism and Empiro-criticism ", and " One Step Forward, Two Steps Back ".

Trotsky : " Terrorism and Communism."

Plekhanov : From his Preface to the Russian translation of Engels' " Socialism Utopian and Scientific ". (Complete Works, vol. XI, p. 88.)

PAGE 76.

Bukharin : " Historic Materialism " : To this book belongs the distinction of reducing Hegelian Marxism to a complete absurdity. Bukharin does not understand the tricks of meta-physics. He does not realize that in order to establish a dialectic philosophy over and above science, it is necessary to accept the mechanical laws of motion just as they are given by the sciences, but at the same time insert into these mechanical laws a set of " speculative " laws, showing that motion is logical *at the same time* that it is mechanical, dialectic *at the same time* that it is dynamic. To put it in Hegel's own words : " The relation of speculative science to the other sciences may be stated in the following terms. It does not in the least neglect the empirical facts contained in the several sciences, but recognizes and adopts them ; it appreciates and applies towards its own structure the universal element in these sciences, their laws and classifications ; but besides all this, into the categories of science it introduces and gives currency to, other categories. . . ." This clever device for the preservation of animism Bukharin does not understand. He thinks that the dialectic laws are themselves mechanical like Newton's laws of motion, or Kepler's or Ein-stein's laws. Thus according to Bukharin we have two mechani-cal sciences side by side—one invented by Hegel and Marx who perhaps never entered a laboratory, and the other developed by men who spent their lives trying to achieve an experimental understanding of mechanical motion. The absurdity of this position is obvious. And it reduces the whole dialectic meta-physics to absurdity, because it is in a sense the same thing naïvely and clumsily done. Bukharin is like the pupil of a magician, giving away the tricks of his master by trying to perform before he has quite learned them.

Lenin : The quotations are from " Materialism and Empiro-criticism ", VI, 4 ; from a letter to Maxim Gorky published in "Pod Znamenem Marxisma "; from his " What to Do ? " II, 2 ; and again from " Materialism and Empiro-criticism ".

PAGE 78.

" Semi-theological jargon " : See Engels' " Feuerbach ", I, and " Landmarks of Scientific Socialism ", p. 152. Also Lenin's " Materialism and Empiro-criticism ", the section on " Absolute and Relative Truth ".

PAGE 79.

I first indicated this view of the relation between Marxism and Freud's psychology in an article on " Wilson and Lenin ", published in " The Liberator " in 1918.

" Infantry, Cavalry and Artillery " : " Der Achtzehnte Brumaire des Louis Bonaparte ", III.

PAGE 82.

Engels : Letter to Franz Mehring, July 14, 1893.

Marx : " Achtzehnte Brumaire ", III.

PAGE 83.

Engels : Letter to Joseph Bloch, September 21, 1890

PAGE 84.

Engels : The quotation is from his letter to Conrad Schmidt, October 27, 1890   The second quotation is from " Feuer-bach ", IV.

PAGE 86.

" An early biographer " : Scott, " Napoleon ", VI, 251. Before Napoleon the word *ideology* meant the science of ideas, and in France—strangely enough—it is this meaning which survives.

PAGE 87.

The quotations are from Engels' " Anti-Dühring ", the chapter on Political Economy, sec. I, and II.

PAGE 88.

The words " more magnificent " occur in the Introduction to " Anti-Dühring ".   " The heavenly bodies like the formations of the organisms by which they are under favourable conditions inhabited, arise and perish, and the courses that they run, so far as is on the whole permissible, take on eternally more magnificent dimensions."

" So often repeated " : Read for instance Engels' Introduction to Marx's " Poverty of Philosophy ", and Marx's " Criticism of the Gotha Program ". This latter document reveals more clearly than any other the manner in which Marx projected his own purpose into the evolving " Economic relations ".

PAGE 91.

Marx : Letter to Engels, January 8, 1868.

PAGE 95.

" Marx himself confessed " : Preface to the second edition of " Das Kapital ".

" Famous subject of dispute " : See Böhm-Bawerk's " Karl Marx and the Close of his System ". The reader will find a defence of Marx's position, in Louis Boudin's book, " The Theoretic System of Karl Marx ", V and VI. I recommend this book as the most reliable outline of orthodox Marxism in English. The book is conceived in a spirit of humorless and unconvincing sarcasm, which will repel the scientific reader—but this also belongs to the orthodox tradition. Marx's " Poverty of Philosophy ", Engels' " Anti-Dühring ", and Plekhanov's attacks upon Mikhaelovsky, were all weakened with this cocksure theological sarcasm. Lenin's polemics are more powerful.

" A penetration " : The quotation is from " Capital ", vol. III, p. 199 of Untermann's translation.

PAGE 96.

Engels : Introduction to Marx's " Wage, Labour and Capital ".

" Experimental humility before the facts themselves " : A step in the direction of this change in Marxian economics has been taken by Karl Renner in his book, " Die Wirtschaft Als Gesamt-Prozess Und Die Sozialisierung ". Conceding that Marx's theory is deductive and abstract in its *mode of exposition*, Renner undertakes to expound it concretely and empirically. So far so good. But until it is conceded that Marx's economics is abstract and deductive—and not only that, but Hegelian-animistic—in its *essential intellectual structure*, the empirical and practical science that is tangled up in it will never be made to emerge clearly.

PAGE 97.

" Inner, hidden " : See page 58 of this book.

" Visible external movement " : " Capital ", vol. III, p. 369, of Untermann's translation.

PAGE 98.

" Independent of their consciousness and their wills " : In his preface to the second edition of " Capital " Marx quotes with approval a Russian critic who says : " Marx regarded the social movement as a process of natural history governed by laws, which are not dependent upon the will, the consciousness or the designs of men, but rather the contrary, which determine their wills, their consciousness and their designs." Marx himself said the same thing in a letter to Annenkov, December 28, 1846. See also " Feuerbach ", IV.

It is surprising how many studious and scientific people have made the mistake of imagining that Marxism rests upon the concept of the " economic man "—Bertrand Russell, for instance (" Roads to Freedom ", p. 47), Paul Howard Douglas in " The Trend of Economics ", p. 154, and the Russian economist, Tugan-Baranovsky. Usually I think this is a result of mere hasty reading. But Tugan-Baranovsky's error was the outcome of a serious effort to understand Marx's mind. He failed in this effort because he took the " Theses on Feuerbach " to mean all that they seem to mean. On the basis of these " Theses ", and of a similar remark in the " Heilige Familie ", he assumed that Marx had abandoned the Hegelian view of the relation between will and understanding, and that " on this decisive psychological point Marx was at one with Schopenhauer and not Hegel ". Having thus erroneously assumed that Marx recognized the primacy of the will, Tugan-Baranovsky naturally proceeded to discover Marx's fundamental error in the fact that he " ignored the many-sidedness " of this will. " Out of all the variegated web of human motives he took into consideration one only, economic interest in the narrowest sense " (" Theoretische Grundlagen des Marxismus ", ch. II, p. 40). Marx did not really take " economic interest " into consideration at all, and therefore Tugan-Baranovsky's whole book is entirely beside the point. Every effort to understand the mind of Marx will be beside the point, which fails to understand that the " Theses on Feuerbach " were a step backward toward Hegel, and not forward with the development of a scientific attitude.

PAGE 99.

The translation is from " Die Heilige Familie ", chapter IV.

PAGE 101.

The translation is from the next to the last chapter of the first volume of " Das Kapital ".

PAGE 103.

" Iron necessity " : The phrase occurs in the Preface to the first edition of " Das Kapital ".

" Hegel's philosophy " : See vol. III, p. 55, of his " Lectures on the History of Philosophy ".

" An association which excludes " : " Das Elend der Philosophie ", II, 5.

PAGE 104.

" Leap from the Kingdom of necessity " : " Anti-Dühring, " III, II.

" Most adequate expression " : Engels' Preface to the first English translation of " Das Kapital ".

PAGE 105.

" Honorific intellectual decoration " : The words are meant to recall the works of Thorstein Veblen, one of the most original revolutionary minds of our time.

That Marx's " Capital " is among the least important of his contributions to the science of revolution, may be seen in the rarity of concrete allusions to its contents among those who are applying the science. It may be seen also in the position occupied by this work in Marx's own life. It was not a preparation for an expected revolution, but a substitute for one which had failed to appear. If Marx's confident expectations in the 'fifties had been fulfilled, we should have had a proletarian dictatorship instead of " Das Kapital ", and the proletariat would have been none the poorer for this difference. These ponderous volumes threw a cloak of honorific intellectualism about the revolutionary movement, disappointed of its first hopes, and that was something of a service in its time. But we know now—thanks to a line of thinking which Marx himself initiated—that the honorific character of a display of pure intellect lies precisely in its futility, which seems to indicate an association with the leisure class. In the name of Marxism itself, we ought to approach such bulky and overpowering parturitions of the " Higher Learning " as " Das Kapital ", with a slight smile of revolutionary satire. For twenty-seven years Marx and Engels withheld the solution of the central difficulty in their theory of value, and for the last decade of this quarter of a century Engels left standing a public

challenge to the scientific world to " guess the answer ".
Whether he and Marx themselves succeeded in guessing the
answer to this riddle, may remain a disputed question. But
there is no questioning their demonstration of the fact that
" Das Kapital " belongs rather to the sphere of noble sports,
than of ignoble utilities.

PAGE 109.

Hegel : The quotation is from his " Philosophy of Religion ".
Engels : The quotations are from the chapter on " Dialectic " in his " Anti-Dühring ".

PAGE 110.

" In another passage " : " Socialism Utopian and Scientific ", II.

PAGE 111.

" A rotten spot " : A good example of what I mean by this
expression will be found in Engels' Introduction to the third
volume of " Capital " (p. 24 of Untermann's translation). He
is discussing the fact that Marx's theory of value, which appears
in the first volume to be a definition and explanation of the
actual normal rates at which commodities exchange on the
market, turns out in the third volume to be a penetration
beneath such superficial phenomena into the " internal essence
and inner form of the capitalist process of production " (p. 199
of the same volume). I have mentioned this difficulty in
Chapter X. What Engels says about it in the spot to which I
allude is this :
" It is a mistaken assumption . . . that one may look at
all in Marx's work for fixed and universally applicable definitions. It is a matter of course that when things and their mutual
inter-relations are conceived, not as fixed, but as changing,
that their mental images the ideas concerning them, are likewise
subject to change and transformation : that they cannot be
sealed up in rigid definitions, but must be developed in the
historical and logical process of their formation."
What seems to me " a matter of course ", is that so long
as you have a philosophy which permits you to dodge out of
difficulties in this irresponsible fashion, real and reliable science
is impossible.
For another example of this employment of the idea of
" dialectic thinking " to dodge a difficulty, see the paragraph
of Engels' letter to Conrad Schmidt, October 27, 1890, beginning, " What these gentlemen lack is dialectic ", and ending,
" For them Hegel never existed ".

PAGE 115.

Lenin : " Once More about the Trade-Unions." Complete Works, vol. XVIII, part I, p. 60.

PAGE 116.

The quotation is from Lenin's article entitled " Concerning Our Revolution ", Complete Works, vol. XIII, part II, p. 117.

PAGE 117.

Marx : Letter to Kugelmann, June 27, 1870.

Engels : Preface to the second edition of " Anti-Dühring ".

Plekhanov : " Cant versus Kant ", Complete Works, XI, p. 41.

PAGE 123.

" Carry it forward " : This does not mean, of course, that Marxians can " make revolutions ", in the catastrophic sense of the word. It would be truer to say that revolutions are a natural force like the tide or the lightning, and just as electrical engineers may be said to have " harnessed the lightning ", so Marxian engineers seek to harness revolutions and make them serve the highest interests of mankind. The distinction, however, between guiding a natural force, and causing it to appear at a given place or moment, is not a precise one, and no man of purpose would dream of founding upon this a dogmatic rule of action. Lenin indicated the natural limits of scientific effort, so far as concerns action in a crisis, in the following words, which he called the Fundamental Law of Revolution :

" Only when the masses do not want the old regime, and when the rulers are unable to govern as of old, only then can a revolution succeed. This truth may be expressed in other words : Revolution is impossible without an all-national crisis, affecting both the exploited and the exploiters."

That such crises will arise in the future, is abundantly proven for all practical purposes by the material assembled in the Marxian economics—if it is not, indeed, obvious to every person who has read history. But Marxian scientists will not confine their efforts to preparing for such economic crises. They will move everything, all the time, in every sphere of life, to the full extent possible in the direction of a proletarian-democratic society.

PAGE 124.

The quotation is from " The Theses on Feuerbach ".

PAGE 130.

Plekhanov : " Anarchism and Socialism." (My translation is from the French text, p. 22.)

PAGE 131.

Kropotkin : " Modern Science and Anarchism ", VIII.

" Ignored the contribution of psychology " : The conclusion of Köhler, for example, in his painstaking study of the behaviour of the chimpanzee, that " Mutual obstruction is more frequent than co-operation ", has a more decisive bearing upon the problem, than all of Kropotkin's more general biological data put together. (" The Mentality of Apes ", by Wolfgang Köhler.)

" Bakunin's early protest " : Mehring's " Life of Marx ", V. 7.

" Bakunin . . . wrote his share " : See for instance, " God and the State " (p. 32 of the New Edition, published by the Freedom Press, 1910): " Whatever human question we may desire to consider, we always find this same essential contradiction between the two schools. Thus, as I have already observed, materialism starts from animality to establish humanity ; idealism starts from divinity to establish slavery and condemn the masses to an endless animality. Materialism denies free will and ends in the establishment of liberty ; idealism, in the name of human dignity, proclaims free will, and on the ruins of every liberty founds authority. Materialism rejects the principle of authority, because it rightly considers it as the corollary of animality, and because, on the contrary, the triumph of humanity, the object and chief significance of history, can be realized only through liberty."

PAGE 132.

Marx : " Das Elend der Philosophie ", II, I.

PAGE 133.

Kropotkin : " Modern Science and Anarchism ", XIII and XV. For another clear statement of what he thinks the science of economics ought to be, see his preface to " Fields, Factories and Workshops ".

PAGE 134.

The three quotations are from Kropotkin's " Modern Science and Anarchism ", IX, XIV, and XII.

In Kropotkin's history of the French Revolution, the reader will see even more clearly the absence of any scientific plan, the reliance upon magic, upon a mystic virtue supposed to reside in what he calls " the people ", to save other revolutions from going the way of this one. He makes it plain that the organization of a centralized state by the middle classes was what prevented the lower classes from gaining any of their ends. But his plan for preventing such a catastrophe in a future revolution is not to organize a corresponding power for the lower classes. His plan is simply and literally to *wish away* that organization of the middle classes. To a practical mind interested in communism, there could be no better argument for the method of proletarian dictatorship than Kropotkin's book, " The Great French Revolution ".

<h3 style="text-align:center">PAGE 135.</h3>

" Any more than the other anarchists " : I dwell upon Kropotkin because, of all the anarchists, he makes the best claim to be considered scientific. The belief in magic is so obvious in the writings of other revolutionary anarchists, that I think it is hardly worth while to demonstrate it. One has only to seek out in each of them the particular event, or idea, or formula, to which he ascribes an occult virtue capable of producing the desired miracle. For Bakunin it was the very idea of " science " taken abstractly which possessed this high potency.

" The major part of the natural laws connected with the development of human society . . . have not been duly recognized and established by science itself.

" Once they shall have been recognized by science, and then from science, by means of an extensive system of popular education and instruction, shall have passed into the consciousness of all, the question of liberty will be entirely solved. The stubbornest authorities must admit that there will be no need either of political organization, or direction, or legislation " (from " God and the State ").

" Seems to the anarchist to be the very obstacle " : This is well illustrated in the writings of Alexander Berkman and Emma Goldman about Soviet Russia. Every person who has learned how to face facts, knows that if it had not been for the Bolshevik organizations, the Russian Revolution would have produced nothing but an ordinary capitalist republic with modern improvements, or, what is perhaps more likely, a limited monarchy. Of this there is not the slightest scientific doubt. Yet these two sincere and devoted people, because they believe in revolutionary magic, go about denouncing the Bolsheviks for having " crushed ", or " dammed up ", some mystic entity which they call " the revolution ", the " rising tide of the people's energies ", the " free creative new humanity ", etc., and prevented it from producing a miraculous transformation of Russian society into " non-governmental anarchist communism ". (See " The Anti-Climax " and " The Bolshevik Myth ", by Alexander Berkman, " The Crushing of the Russian Revolution ", etc., by Emma Goldman.)

PAGE 137.

George Sorel : The quotations are from " La Décomposition du Marxisme ", VI, and " Réflexions sur la Violence ", IV, III.

PAGE 139.

" The longest backward step taken by any genuinely revolutionary theorist " : A longer backward step, and a somewhat similar one, has recently been taken by Hendrik de Man, a former Marxist, in a book called " Zur Psychologie des Sozialismus ", but De Man cannot be described as a genuinely revolutionary theorist. Sorel worked out a metaphysical consecration of the present motive in order to get the support of the universe in his revolutionary purpose. De Man has worked out a similar, although more mystical, consecration of *mere* motive, in order to get religious support for his abandonment of the revolutionary purpose.

" The older I grow," he confesses, " the more I feel myself a revolutionist, but the less I believe in the revolution. I am a revolutionist : that means that the transformation of capitalism into a socialist order is to me a psychical motive. . . . The present motive, not the future goal, is the sole essential. . . . I am a socialist, not because I believe in the superiority of the socialist image of the future over any other ideal, but because I have the conviction that the socialist motive makes better and happier men. . . . It is a perspectival delusion of our will which, so to speak, sifts out socialism from the activities of the present moment, in order to misplace it as a ' goal ' in the future. Goals are only imaginary points of a future horizon, upon which we project the desired end of our volitional tendency. . . . If socialism as a movement has any general meaning, it is to make the men who take part in this movement happier. . . . The essential thing in socialism is the struggle for it. . . . I believe still only in the revolution which transforms our Self. This conception corresponds as well to the demands of *real-political* opportunity as to those of the moral law. . . . This same conviction that the ethical motive is at the same time the best and only *real-politic*, guides me when I emphasize the necessity of a regeneration of the socialist attitude through the moral-religious consciousness. . . . There is nothing more real in man than the divine power of the moral law."

It is needless to prove that this talk is not scientific, since it quite frankly declares itself religious. What I am moved to say about it, is that it is immoral. All that there is in me which corresponds to those words " ethical motive ", " moral law ", etc.—namely a strong sense of what is good and praiseworthy in human character and conduct—finds this abandonment of purposive intelligence in behalf of mere emotional motive, bad and weak and sickly, and to be condemned unconditionally by every person who loves humanity or has any hope of its development.

Unfortunately De Man has united this reactionary movement of his character with some valid criticisms of Marxism from the standpoint of modern psychology. He has correctly detected the concealment of the wish in orthodox Marxism. But since he does not understand the specific historical and cultural reasons why Marx's mind produced this tangle, he cannot find the scientific way out. He only succeeds in building up, on a very thin scaffolding of old-fashioned psychological ideas, another mythology, a story about various " stages " in the development of an effort of creative imagination—pure utopian, practical-utopian, practico-rational utopian, and then practico-ethical, which is the name for his own stage. It would not take Marx three minutes to point out the essential fact, namely that this " practico-ethical stage " in the development of the revolution is nothing but an ideological disguise for the abandonment of the revolutionary purpose.

De Man's book became known to me only after my own book had gone to the publisher, and I cannot extensively discuss his " Psychology of Socialism ". I insert this note at the last moment, merely to indicate my general opinion. De Man does not understand the mind of Marx, and he does not understand that " psychological science of science ", from the standpoint of which he professes to criticize Marxism.

" Reason, hopes and the perception " : " Réflexions sur la Violence ", IV, p. 181.

PAGE 142.

Lenin : " What to do ? ", IV, 3.

PAGE 143.

The quotation is from Lenin's Introduction to the first edition of a collection of articles entitled " After Twelve Years " written in 1907.

" Official history " : " A History of the Russian Communist Party ", by Gregory Zinoviev, p. 71, of the Russian Edition, Moscow, 1923.

PAGE 144.

" Lenin repeatedly declared " : In " What to Do ? " the statement occurs three times. My quotation is from chap. IV, sec. 3.

The quotations are all from " What to Do ? "

PAGE 147.

Plekhanov : " The Working Class and the Social Democratic Intelligentsia ", an article in " Iskra ", No. 71, August 1,
1904. Plekhanov's citation from Marx is from " The Holy
Family ". Lenin's tribute to Plekhanov's philosophical writings
is in the article already cited, " Once more About the Trade
Unions ", and his response to Plekhanov's attack appears in
the Introduction to " After 12 Years ".

PAGE 149.

" Midwife of Revolution " : " We are not utopians . . .
we are men of science, we do not devise new social forms, but
only offer to capitalist society the service of midwife, when the
hour comes for the birth of a socialist society." (Paul Lafargue
in a Debate with Jaurès.)

PAGE 151.

" Better that ten workers " : The quotation is from the
official report of the second convention of the Russian Social-
Democratic Workers' Party, in London, 1903 (p. 251).

" Attempted to define them " : Karl Radek describes this
change in Lenin's way of thinking as an advance in scientific
accuracy. He says that Lenin " did not at first understand the
social significance and social sources " of Menshevism. For
that reason he first emphasized the distinction between " reasoners and fighters " within the working class. Subsequently
he learned to identify Menshevism with the new layers of the
petty bourgeoisie which are constantly entering the proletariat.
And at a still later date he regarded it as " the politics of that
part of the working class which can find satisfaction for its
interests inside the frame of bourgeois society ",—that is, the
aristocracy of labour. Radek fails to note that Lenin never
abandoned his original psychological definition, but kept it
going *alongside of* these new economic ones. How strongly
it survives in authoritative circles, may be seen in the statement
of Clara Zetkin at the Fifth Congress of the Communist International, that " the organizational and political superiority of
Bolshevism . . . is the principle that a revolutionary party
cannot tolerate merely paying members, that every member
must be an active, working, fighting member ". A science of
revolution must reconcile these two entirely different ways

of approaching this important problem, and it seems to me there is only one truthful way to do it. Lenin's original statement was a correct definition of the distinction between Bolshevik and Menshevik: these subsequent statements were formulations of what made Menshevik intellectuals particularly dangerous at certain epochs to the proletarian revolution. (My quotations are from Radek's articles on " The Scientific Organization of Labour in the Perspective of the Further Development of the Revolution ", beginning in *Pravda*, No. 41, 1924.)

PAGE 152.

" Work, according to the definition of Marx " : " Das Kapital ", vol. I, sec. 3, ch. V.

PAGE 156.

The quotation is from " What to Do ? ", IV, 3.

" He was seriously attacked " : Speech* of Akimov in the Second Congress of the Russian Social Democratic Labour Party in 1903. The quotation immediately following is from Lenin's pamphlet " The Infantile Disease of Leftism ", VI.

PAGE 157.

" Veritable tribunes of the people " : These quotations are also from " What to Do ? ".

" Marx also recognized the peasants " : In a letter to Engels, often cited by Lenin himself, Marx wrote : " The whole cause of Germany will depend upon the possibility of reinforcing the proletarian revolution with a kind of second edition of the Peasants' War, then all will be well." (Translated from Lenin's text.)

PAGE 158.

" Policy of sharp turns " : The expression is used by Trotsky in " The New Course ".

PAGE 160.

" Pausing to write a tribute to Lenin " : Bukharin's " Lenin, Marxist " is a fair example of these orthodox writings. After a conscientious but pale account of certain modifications introduced by Lenin in the Marxian theory, Bukharin casually mentions his " teaching upon the organization and structure of the party, the relations among the party, the working class, the masses, the leaders, etc.", calling this a "secondary question".

A pamphlet of Karl Radek, "About Lenin", contains some marked contrasts to this orthodox way of approaching Lenin. "The principal science of Lenin as a political leader preparing the conquest of power by the proletariat, was his science of the significance of the proletarian party." "The greatness of Lenin consisted in the fact that no formula composed yesterday ever prevented him from seeing the changing reality, that he had the courage to abandon yesterday's formula if it prevented his grasping to-day's reality."

PAGE 161.

The quotation is from " The Infantile Disease of Leftism "

PAGE 163.

The quotation is from Lenin's article " Concerning Our Revolution ", Complete Works, vol. XVIII, part 2, p. 118 ff.

PAGE 164.

The quotations from Marx are to be found in the Introduction to the " Critique of Political Economy ", " The Poverty of Philosophy ", II, 5, the " Criticism of the Gotha Program " and the Preface to the first edition of " Capital".

PAGE 166.

The passage from Cardinal Manning is quoted by Lytton Strachey in his " Eminent Victorians ".

PAGE 167.

" Truth is always concrete " : A favourite maxim with both Lenin and Plekhanov, quoted from Chernishevsky, who first introduced the Hegelian philosophy into Russian revolutionary circles.

" Marx says " : Letter to Weidemeier, March 5, 1852.

" Lenin says " : " State and Revolution."

PAGE 168.

" In Lenin the scientific thinker " : The doubleness of Marx's mental character, and the singleness of Lenin's, were both observed by those who knew them. H. M. Hyndman described most vividly the interplay between the purposive thinker and the metaphysical professor in Marx. " The contrast," he wrote, " between his excitement in moments of strong indignation and the peaceful transition to an exposition of his views on contemporary economic events was most striking. He passed without visible effort from the rôle of prophet and flaming prosecutor to the rôle of tranquil philosopher. . . ." (Re-translated from a foreign text.) Compare what Trotsky says about Lenin : " This great engineer of history, not only in politics, but in his theoretical works, in his philosophical speculations, in the study of foreign languages, and in conversation with people, was continually possessed by one and the same idea—the goal."

PAGE 169.

Engels : " Anti-Dühring ", I, XI. " How young is all human history, and how ridiculous it would be, to wish to ascribe any absolute validity to our present views, may be inferred from the simple fact that all history up to now may be described as the history of the period from the practical discovery of the transformation of mechanical motion into heat, until that of the transformation of heat into mechanical motion."

Lenin : " Materialism and Empiro-criticism ", VI, 2. The second quotation is from " What to Do ? "

PAGE 170.

The quotation is from " Materialism and Empiro-criticism ", VI, 2.

PAGE 172.

" Partisan " : " Materialism and Empiro-criticism ", VI, 4, and " Conclusion ".

PAGE 176.

" This is the period " : The quotation, if I remember rightly, is the first sentence of the first " Manifesto " of the Third International.

PAGE 178.

Bukharin and Pavlov : *Krasnaia Nov*, January, February and March 1924.

" Only the final science " : The quotation is from Pavlov's " Twenty Years' Experience ".

PAGE 179.

Hegel : " Logic ", p. 103.

PAGE 180.

Lenin : " Pod Znamenem Marxisma ", No. 2, and " Materialism and Empiro-Criticism ", VI, 4.

PAGE 181.

Bakunin : " God and the State ", p. 44.

PAGE 182.

The statement that " Religion is the opium of the people ", occurs in Marx's " Introduction to a Criticism of Hegel's Philosophy of Law ". (" Nachlass ", vol. I, p. 385.)

PAGE 183.

" Recent Manifesto from Moscow " : published in " L'Humanité," October 13, 1924.

" The only ultimate distinction " : See my " Enjoyment of Poetry ".

PAGE 186.

Lenin : *Pod Znamenem Marxisma*, No. 3, 1922.

In connection with this page I will mention another slight advantage which may accrue to revolutionary art from a disestablishment of the religion of Marxism. A certain liberty of opinion may be allowed as to whether Marx himself was a great artist.   Franz Mehring—a person of general literary culture and discrimination—says in his biography (VIII, 2) that " Marx might compete in striking figurativeness of language with the great masters of comparison, Lessing, Goethe, Hegel ". And among orthodox Marxists this is a very general opinion.

Here is an example of the way in which Marx used comparison—one of the worst examples, to be sure, but still taken from his mature, and not his youthful writings. He is speaking of the allotment of land to the peasants in France

" The bourgeois order, which at the beginning of the century had placed the state as a sentry before the newly arisen allotment and dunged it with laurels, has become a vampire, which sucks out its heart's blood and brain-matter and throws it in the Alchemist's retort of capital." (" Achtzehnte Brumaire ", pp. 101, 102, of the third edition.)

Nobody who knew the first principles of the art of comparison could have written this sentence. Marx had in his head the materials of which great literature is composed, but he lacked the fineness of imaginative perception and feeling to make any consistent use of them. He did indeed write some great sentences—but only a few, and never when he tried to.

PAGE 188.

Lenin : The quotations are from " What to Do ? " and " The Infantile Disease of Leftism ".

PAGE 189.

Bernstein : See " Evolutionary Socialism " and " Socialism and Science ".

PAGE 191.

" Increasing misery " : This theory belonged solely to the metaphysical construction of Marx. How little he cared about it as a practical man may be seen in one of his own matter-of-fact remarks : " As to the working-classes, it is still a much debated question whether their condition has been bettered at all as a result of the growth of the so-called public wealth ". (" Poverty of Philosophy ", I, III.)

PAGE 194.

" The theorists of the present British Communist party " : Eden and Cedar Paul, in their " Creative Revolution ", show the keenest consciousness of the problem of reconciling Marxism with Anglo-Saxon ways of thinking, and they make the most thoughtful effort to do it. But even they only succeed in denying that Marxism is what it is.

The following quotation from the " Communist Review ", vol. II, No. 4, will give the official theoretic position of the British party.

" First to clear away a misconception. The term Materialism has no connection with philosophic materialism in the absolute and final sense . . . Eden and Cedar Paul in their ' Creative Revolution ' write :

" ' Historical Materialism is quite distinct from philosophic materialism. . . . Marx did not assert, as do the materialists in the philosophic meaning of the term, that the only real things in the universe are matter and motion. . . .'

" Again Harry Waton, an American Marxist, says :

" ' The philosophy of Marx is not an ontology : it is not a philosophy of the universe, it does not attempt to explain the ultimate nature of things . . . the philosophy of Marx is the philosophy of human society.' "

That is British Marxism. And here is Russian Marxism :

" Marxism—this is a complete world-view. Expressing it briefly, it is *contemporary materialism*, representing the highest stage of development in the present time of that view of the world, the foundations of which were laid in ancient Greece by Democritus, and in part by the Ionic thinkers who preceded

him : the so-called *hylozoism* is nothing but naïve *materialism*.
. . The historic and economic sides of this world-view . . .
are almost exclusively the work of Marx and Engels. . . .
The term Marxism often designates only these two sides of
the contemporary materialistic world-view. These two sides
are regarded in that case as something completely independent
of ' philosophic materialism ', if not even opposite to it. And
since these two sides, arbitrarily torn from the context of
opinions which is native to them, and which constitutes their
theoretical foundation, cannot remain hanging in the air,
there naturally arises among people who have perpetrated such
an uprooting operation upon them, a demand that Marxism
should be ' founded' over again. . . ." (Plekhanov : " Fundamental Problems of Marxism ", pp. 1–2. His own italics.)

" Consciousness in general reflects existence—that is the
general proposition of *all* materialism. It is impossible not to
see its direct and *uninterrupted* connection with the proposition of historic materialism, social consciousness *reflects* social
existence." (Lenin, " Materialism and Empiro-criticism ", VI, 2.
His own italics.)

" That Marxism really is what it is " : Vladimir Simkhovitch's book, " Marxism versus Socialism ", consists essentially
in telling Anglo-Saxon socialists who do not know it, that
Marxism is not a practical hypothesis, but a system of objective
belief about the necessary course of history. Simkhovitch
assembles the principal points which have been advanced to
show that such a belief is unscientific, and adds some shrewd
comments of his own. If he stopped there, his work, so far as
it goes, would be unassailable. But he tried to infer from this
that the social revolution is an impossibility. " If certain conditions and tendencies make socialism inevitable," he asks,
" do not the absence of these conditions and the existence of
contrary tendencies make socialism impossible ? " If the
contrary tendencies were forceful and overwhelming, this
question would arrest attention. But as an argument under
the existing circumstances, the only way in which it could be
made cogent would be to supply the major premise : " Everything which is not inevitable is impossible." And this would
give us a universe even more rigidly determined than that
Marxian one which Simkhovitch ridicules. Simkhovitch tried
to replace Marx's revolutionary ideology of the necessity of
socialism, with a counter-revolutionary ideology of its impossibility. Both these ideologies are inconsistent with practical
scientific thought and effort, and having dismissed the one, we
need not occupy ourselves with the other.

260 THE SCIENCE OF SOCIAL REVOLUTION

PAGE 195.

" The belief in ideas " : This psychological definition of Menshevism, although written originally for this book, was first published in my " Leon Trotsky, the Portrait of a Youth ".

PAGE 198.

Kautsky : " The Dictatorship of the Proletariat ", X.

Lenin : " Kautsky, the Renegade ", VIII.

" I am not a Marxist ! " : See Franz Mehring's " Life of Karl Marx ", XV, 6 ; Charles Longuet's Preface to his French translation of " The Civil War in France ", or " Die Neue Zeit " for 1900-1, p. 427 of the first volume.

" Wilhelm Liebknecht " : See his letter to Marx, published n *Pravda*, March 28, 1926.

Lenin : See part II, chap. IV of this book.

Trotsky : " Lessons of October ", p. XLII ; " War and Revolution ",pp. 322, 323 ; " The New Course ", p. 85 ; " Lessons of October ", p. XVII.

PAGE 199.

Karl Radek : " The development of Socialism from Science to Practice " (Translation published by the Socialist Labour Press in Glasgow, pp. 14, 15).

PAGE 202.

Hegel : " Logic ", p. 51.

Engels : Preface to the second edition of " Anti-Dühring ".

" His American translator " : Austin Lewis (see " Landmarks of Scientific Socialism ", Appendix p. 261).

Kautsky : " Three Crises in Marxism ". " For the understanding of Marx," he says, " a certain knowledge is required, and a tireless striving to penetrate deeper and deeper. At first acquaintance one always understands Marxism cheaply and vulgarly ; it is necessary continually to increase the stores of one's knowledge, and with the newly acquired knowledge tackle again and again the study of Marx's works, for only then is it possible to understand and solve the contradiction between the surface and the essence of things, between their superficially apparent and their profound relations." (From a Russian text.)

PAGE 203.

Plekhanov : " A new condition of the productive forces

brings after it a new economic structure, as well as a new psychology, a new spirit of the times. From this it is evident that only in popular speech is it permissible to speak of economy as the *primary cause* of all social phenomena. Far from being the primary cause, it is itself a consequence, a ' function ' of the productive forces ". " The Question of the Development of a Monistic View of History ", V.

Lenin : " Once More about the Trade-Unions ", Complete Works, vol. XVIII, part I, p. 60.

PAGE 204.

" The eloquence of Bakunin " : " God and the State ' " It is time," he says, " to have done with all popes and priests ; we want them no longer, even if they call themselves Social-Democrats."

PAGE 205.

" Seeking for contradictions in capitalism " : The advice of N. Bukharin in an article published in " The Workers' Monthly ", Chicago, 1925.

PAGE 206.

" Reflection in the heads of Marxists " : The quotation is from a pamphlet by Sarabianov entitled " Historical Materialism ".

PAGE 208.

Marx   " The Poverty of Philosophy ".

Plekhanov : " Anarchism and Socialism " : (From the French text, p. 22).

PAGE 209.

Engels : " Landmarks of Scientific Socialism ", p. 221.

" The population of Russia " : According to a census report printed in " L'Humanité ", December 1925.

PAGE 212.

Lenin : " Infantile Disease of Leftism ", VI, and " State and Revolution ", VI, 3.

Bertrand Russell : " Roads to Freedom ", VIII. Although he gave his book this very promising title, " Roads to Freedom ", Bertrand Russell never for the length of one sentence took the view-point of a man standing in a defined position in the present, and asking the scientific question : With what forces, and by what method of their employment, can I begin actually moving in the desired direction ? His book, like all anarchistic writings, is about " Programmes of Freedom "—a valuable contribution to that discussion, indeed the first contribution which shows the influence of modern psychology. But Bertrand Russell's programmes are left hanging in the air, as though they might realize themselves by the mere act of their promulgation. That is why I describe him as an extreme utopian from the point of view of method.

A similar thing is to be said of Thorstein Veblen's book " Engineers and the Price System ", which purports to be practically scientific.

PAGE 213.

" Confused figure " : My translation is from the French of Victor Serge, who quotes this sentence in his " Lenin—1917 ". It is amusing to note that Trotsky's more visual mind is troubled by this figure, and in reproducing it from memory he instinctively tries to improve it. " Lenin, I think, first expressed in 'Iskra' the thought that in the complicated chain of political activity one must know how to pick out the link that is central for the given moment, so that seizing it one may give direction to the whole chain " (" About Lenin ", V). Trotsky's improvement consists of detaching the chain from its fastening in the future, and converting it into something more in the nature of an armoured car !

Trotsky, as I have shown, is none too orthodox. He makes a more scrupulous effort to be orthodox than Lenin did. He lacks the philosophic self-confidence of his leader, and he is more conscious of the intellectual difficulties in their position. Also he finds the true theological way out. " The will to revolutionary activity," he says, in a pamphlet on Communism and Education, " is a condition indispensable to the understanding of the Marxian dialectic "—which is not far from saying, " All your doubts will disappear after you join the church ".

" In six months " : See Trotsky's " About Lenin ", V.

" What socialism will be " : From the Stenographic Report of the Seventh Congress of the Russian Communist Party, Fifth Session, March 8, 1918.

PAGE 214.

" Permanent Revolution " : " The proletariat is gathering more and more to the standard of revolutionary socialism, of communism, for which the bourgeoisie itself has found the name of Blanqui. This socialism is the declaration of a Permanent Revolution, the class-dictatorship of the proletariat, as a necessary transition-period to the abolition of all class-distinctions, and of all the relations of production upon which they rest, of all the social conditions which correspond to these relations of production, and to the revolutionizing of all the ideas which arise from these social conditions." (Karl Marx. " Die Klassenkämpfe in Frankreich : 1848–1850 ", pp. 94, 95.)

INDEX

DATE DUE

NOV 0 5 1996			